READING DIAGNOSIS
AND REMEDIATION

ERIC / CRIER Reading Review Series

SERIES EDITOR, Edward G. Summers, *Indiana University*

A. STERL ARTLEY:
Trends and Practices in Secondary School Reading, 1968

RUTH STRANG:
Reading Diagnosis and Remediation, 1968

ROGER FARR:
Reading: What Can be Measured?

These IRA *Research Fund Monographs are available from the* INTERNATIONAL READING ASSOCIATION, *Six Tyre Avenue, Newark, Delaware 19711.*

Reading diagnosis and remediation

Ruth Strang, Ontario Institute for Studies in Education

The ERIC Clearinghouse on Retrieval of Information and Evaluation on Reading is a joint project of the International Reading Association and Indiana University in cooperation with the Educational Resources Information Center of the U.S. Office of Education. The development of the manuscript for this volume was supported through a contract with the United States Department of Health, Education, and Welfare. Publication was made possible through a grant from the International Reading Association Research Fund.

International Reading Association Research Fund

Newark, Delaware 1968

Second Printing, March 1971

Reading Diagnosis and Remediation was prepared pursuant to a contract with the Office of Education, U. S. Department of Health, Education, and Welfare. Contractors undertaking such projects under Government sponsorship are encouraged to express freely their judgment in professional and technical matters. Points of view or opinions do not, therefore, necessarily represent official Office of Education position or policy.

The International Reading Association attempts, through its publications, to provide a forum for a wide spectrum of opinion on reading. This policy permits divergent viewpoints without assuming the endorsement of the Association.

CONTENTS

FOREWORD

The creation of ERIC (Educational Resources Information Center) and its 18 decentralized information centers has been documented in various publications of the USOE and through the information retrieval centers now in operation around the country. The reader is referred to publications of the U. S. Office and the Clearinghouses for details of how ERIC began, how it has gone about its work, where it stands at the moment, and future plans being laid for information retrieval and analysis activities in education. A list of the eighteen current ERIC information centers is supplied at the end of this foreword. The interested reader can contact any of these centers for detailed information on ERIC activities.

One idea that has remained paramount throughout the planning and development of ERIC is the concept that an information facility developed to serve the broad needs of education should almost immediately become involved in the analysis and interpretation of information as well as its collection, organization, and dissemination. Herein lies one of the strengths of the decentralized as opposed to the centralized information system. In such a system, possibilities for interaction between the professional groups related to the various domains of education and the relevant data are necessarily increased.

Information analysis can take place on a broad continuum ranging from comprehensive reviews of the state of the knowledge in a given area to bibliographies of citations on various topics. *The Reading Review Series* of the ERIC Clearinghouse on Retrieval of Information and Evaluation on Reading has been created to disseminate its information analysis products. Four genres of documents appear in the series. The first type includes bibliographies with descriptive abstracts in areas of general interest. The second type consists of bibliographies of citations, or citations and abstracts, developed on more specific topics in reading. The third type provides short, interpretive papers which analyze specific topics in reading using the existing information collection. The final genre includes comprehensive state-of-the-art monographs which critically examine given topics in reading over an extended period of time.

Ruth Strang's state-of-the-art monograph makes a significant contribution to the field of reading. Its importance as a reference work in the training and preparation of clinicians and specialists is obvious as is its usefulness as a source for the researcher. *Reading Diagnosis and Remediation* is unique in that it also is designed as a practical guide for the teacher or diagnostician—it clearly delineates those practices which research has indicated as being of value and which are applicable at the classroom level. The text also provides an evaluation of diagnostic tools and procedures while the appendix lists those tests useful for diagnostic purposes.

The field of diagnosis and remediation appears at times to be extremely confusing to the researcher. Much of this can be attributed to seemingly uncontrollable variables operating in the reading process itself as well as to the diversity of reported research findings. Herein lies the unique contribution of Ruth Strang's work. Seldom before has the enormous disparity and quantity of research in diagnosis and remediation been integrated and synthesized so systematically. While no one theory or system of practice is generally accepted, Strang has been able to glean those practices which have a proven value. She, however, is quick to point out that no pat solutions can be expected or, indeed, are possible to the problems related to theory and practice in diagnosis and remediation. The final chapter of the monograph provides a cogent discussion of trends, needs, and future directions for research in the field. ERIC/CRIER is pleased to publish *Reading Diagnosis and Remediation* as the second of its comprehensive state-of-the-art monographs in the Reading Review Series.

Edward G. Summers
Project Director
ERIC/CRIER

THE EIGHTEEN CLEARINGHOUSES IN THE ERIC SYSTEM

ADULT EDUCATION
Syracuse University
107 Roney Lane
Syracuse, N. Y. 13210

COUNSELING & PERSONNEL
SERVICES
Services Information Center
611 Church St.
Ann Arbor, Michigan 48104

URBAN DISADVANTAGED
Teachers College
Columbia University
New York, N. Y. 10027

EARLY CHILDHOOD EDUCATION
University of Illinois
805 West Pennsylvania Ave.
Urbana, Ill. 61801

EDUCATIONAL
ADMINISTRATION
University of Oregon
Eugene, Oregon 97403

EDUCATIONAL FACILITIES
University of Wisconsin
606 State St.
Madison, Wis. 53703

EDUCATIONAL MEDIA &
TECHNOLOGY
Institute for Communication
Research
Stanford University
Palo Alto, Calif. 94305

EXCEPTIONAL CHILDREN
National Education
Association
1201 16th St., N.W.
Washington, D. C. 20036

JUNIOR COLLEGE
INFORMATION
University of California at
Los Angeles
405 Hilgard Ave.
Los Angeles, Calif. 90024

LIBRARY & INFORMATION
SCIENCES
University of Minnesota
2122 Riverside Ave.
Minneapolis, Minn. 55404

LINGUISTICS
Center for Applied Linguistics
1717 Massachusetts Ave.,
N.W.
Washington, D. C. 20036

READING
Indiana University
200 Pine Hall
Bloomington, Ind. 47401

RURAL EDUCATION & SMALL
SCHOOLS
Box AP, University Park
Branch
New Mexico State University
Las Cruces, N. Mex. 88001

SCIENCE EDUCATION
Ohio State University
1460 West Lane Ave.
Columbus, Ohio 43221

TEACHER EDUCATION
1156 15th Street, N.W.
Washington, D. C. 20005

TEACHING OF ENGLISH
National Council of Teachers
of English
508 South Sixth St.
Champaign, Ill. 61820

TEACHING OF FOREIGN
LANGUAGES
Modern Language Assoc. of
America
62 Fifth Ave.
New York, N. Y. 10011

VOCATIONAL & TECHNICAL
EDUCATION
Ohio State University
980 Kinnear Road
Columbus, Ohio 43212

PREFACE

The diagnostic *process* has been relatively unexplored by research methods. Most of the articles have been descriptive. The research available is largely concerned with the relation of many physical, neurological, psychological, and social factors to reading achievement, too often measured by only one or two standardized tests. Still fewer articles have described remedial measures in detail and given adequate evidence of their efficacy.

It would be desirable if, from the research reported, we could arrive at a hierarchy of relationships among the correlates of reading disability. At present this is impossible because the investigators have used different populations, different research designs, different instruments of measurement, and different criteria of reading achievement. However, this inability to generalize may be less important than is generally assumed. A teacher or clinician needs to know the relationship of certain factors to reading achievement of the individual or group with whom he is working. In a sense, each research effort that specifically describes the group studied, the method used, and the results obtained is providing differentiated norms for other groups of the same kind.

It would be quite possible to write a separate monograph on each of the topics included in this review of diagnosis and remediation. This monograph attempts only to explore the nature and levels of diagnosis, the correlates and causes of reading achievement and disability, diagnostic techniques, the problem of diagnosis in special groups, and remedial practices. The reviewing of this area was exhausting but far from exhaustive. It seemed more useful, in the space available, to describe a smaller number of studies in some detail than to try to "cover" a larger number of articles.

It is hoped that the monograph will be useful to reading teachers and clinicians. It should give them a point of view regarding diagnosis leading to remediation; alert them to correlates and causes of reading difficulties; acquaint them with a large number of broad coverage tests, batteries, and more specific diagnostic tests that enable diagnosticians to move from labels such as reading retardation to more precise diagnostic hypotheses.

Ruth Strang

1. *Introduction*

An understanding of the reading process is essential to effective diagnosis of reading problems. Viewed as a communication process, reading involves the abilities *1*] to decode or decipher the author's printed words; *2*] to invest them with meaning acquired through the reader's first-hand experience and previous reading; and *3*] to express the ideas thus acquired through speaking, drawing, writing, or other motor responses. Kirk (1962) traces this process from intake to output. At the intake end is the process of decoding or recognizing words. In the association area, meaning is derived from the symbols recognized. At the output end, the reader expresses the significance of the selection through verbal and motor channels.

Diagnosis, in a sense, parallels the reading process from intake to output. Since oral language is primary and prerequisite to reading, information should be obtained about the individual's speech and oral expression. Visual and auditory acuity make receptivity of the visual impression possible. The visual impression acquires meaning through the process of perception. Perceptions, then, are integrated into concepts and more complex thought patterns or schema. The comprehension of the printed words produces final verbal or motor expression. Influencing every stage of this process are general mental ability, emotional factors, the individual's self-concept, and environmental and cultural conditions. All these may facilitate or inhibit his reading development. Thus, diagnosis is concerned with as comprehensive and detailed a description as possible of the reading development and difficulties of groups and, especially, individuals in perceiving, relating, and expressing thoughts written on the printed page.

Frequency of reading disabilities

Estimates of the frequency of reading disabilities vary greatly, depending upon the definition and type of reading disability, the population sampled, the tests used, the statistical methods employed, and the investigator's interpretation of what constitutes a reading disability. The incidence of severe reading disability now usually called dyslexia, and less often designated as "congenital word blindness," in the school population has been estimated as from less than 1 per cent to 4.5 per cent. The frequency of reading disabilities as defined by psychologists has been estimated as from ten to forty per cent. If the point at which a reading disability is said to occur is set on the distribution of reading scores below one sigma, 13.3 to 20.8 per cent of the school population would be classified as disabled readers; of those above 100 I.Q., 4.9 per cent; and of those above 90 I.Q., 8.5 per cent. In general, estimates range from 10 to 25 per cent of the school population.

According to M. D. Vernon (1960), surveys have not reported:

the amount of severe permanent backwardness.

How many children, apart from low-grade defectives, never learn at all? And how many learn just enough to read simple notices and instructions, the betting news and the football pools, but cannot read a continuous text? This information should not be impossible to obtain, but until we have it, we cannot tell whether illiteracy is still a serious problem in this country; whether or not the current methods of teaching are about as effective as they can be. (1960, p. 147)

The nature of diagnosis

The words *identification, assessment, appraisal, evaluation,* and *diagnosis* have this in common: they all attempt to understand how well an individual reads. Identification is the narrowest of these and also the most common practice. But ascertaining the level of an individual's reading performance or locating a reading problem is only the first step. *Assessment, appraisal, evaluation,* and *diagnosis* go further than merely recognizing status and difficulty. The term diagnosis, as used by Bateman (1965), includes three other steps: *1*] noting discrepancy between the individual's expected or potential and his actual level of performance, *2*] describing his reading behavior as completely and specifically as possible, and *3*] determining probable causes and relevant correlates of his present reading performance. Diagnosis, as viewed in this monograph, includes study of the conditions within the individual and in his environment that may explain his reading development.

In the diagnostic process, the worker obtains information from the client, interprets and synthesizes it. He tries to understand the individual in his own terms, in relation to his own meanings and values. Then, he uses this understanding to develop his strengths and overcome his weaknesses. Thus, diagnosis leads directly to remedial action; they go hand in hand, each contributing to the other.

It is the present writer's point of view (Strang, 1964) that diagnosis should have a positive emphasis, be continuous and conterminous with instruction, as well as interwoven with treatment. It should include consideration of relevant ecological as well as personal factors and recognize multiple causes and correlates of reading development and disability. The earlier unfavorable factors are recognized, the greater is the chance of preventing failure.

Diagnosis underlies prevention as well as remediation of reading difficulties: it makes possible a diagnostic curriculum, based on an understanding of the student's capacity, previous knowledge, difficulties, interests, attitudes, and values. Such understanding leads to diagnostic teaching, which makes individualized instruction possible by knowledge of appropriate experiences to provide for each student.

In working with individual cases, diagnosis is a systematic way of finding out the student's abilities and deficits and what is facilitating or inhibiting his progress. Diagnosis leads to hypotheses, and hypotheses lead directly to remedial planning.

The relationship between clinical diagnostic and remedial procedures is represented schematically by Bateman (1965, p. 177). The four main diagnostic steps already mentioned are paralleled by remedial measures using all the techniques and materials available to give instruction and practice in the strengths and weaknesses uncovered. This initial direct attack on the reading difficulties as the individual presents them will be broadened to include related areas of reading performance and behavioral aspects. Various word attack skills, aspects of comprehension, and other reading competencies will be taught as the need is recognized.

Diagnosis on different levels

Diagnosis of reading disabilities may be made on different levels of comprehensiveness, psychological depth, and competence (Strang, 1964a, pp. 3-23). On the surface level, the effort is made to describe reading performance—strengths and weaknesses in vocabulary, word recognition, sentence and paragraph comprehension, and related abilities. These kinds of information may be obtained during classroom instruction and from informal and standardized reading tests (Strang, 1965b). The teacher can use this information immediately to reinforce strengths and minimize weaknesses. Thus, education can proceed without a prolonged preliminary definitive diagnosis. To measure teachers' ability to do this, Burnett (1963) constructed a problem-solving reading test based on problems similar to those encountered in the classroom. It consisted of multiple-choice exercises, each exercise representing a different degree of adequacy in the solution of the stated problem. The test's validity was indicated by statistically significant differences among groups of undergraduates, experienced teachers, and reading teachers.

On a second level, clues to other aspects of the pupil's behavior that influence his reading performance can be observed or ascertained through interviews and personality tests. For example, the teacher or clinician may note a general passivity or low energy level that may be preventing a student from putting forth the effort that reading demands. Or a meager speaking vocabulary, imprecise articulation, immature sentence structure, and other inadequacies in verbal communication could make it difficult for another student to decode and interpret reading material. Without this oral vocabulary, he would not know the meaning of a word even though he pronounced it correctly. Anxiety may interfere with the individual's thought processes. Observation of the student's habits of work—a tendency to give up when the task is difficult, intermittent spurts of effort followed by periods of indolence, lack of concern for accuracy, an "anything goes" attitude (often labeled "carelessness")—may give important clues to factors that may be influencing a student's reading performance.

A third level of diagnosis attempts to analyze the student's reading process rather than merely to describe his reading performance. This may be done systematically in the Illinois Test of Psycholinguistic Abilities (ITPA). In this test, the reading process is described from intake to output through the steps of reception, perception, differentiation, association, retention, and retrieval leading to motor, visual, or vocal output. In such a differential diagnosis, specific strengths and deficiencies can be detected and necessary remedial measures, instruction, and practice can be given.

A fourth level of reading diagnosis is concerned with other mental abilities underlying success in reading such as visual-memory and association. These abilities are suggested by subtest scores on the Wechsler Intelligence Scale for Children (WISC) or the Wechsler Adult Intelligence Scale (WAIS). Some of these abilities are similar to those detected by the ITPA. Others are more subtle and pervasive aspects of memory and reasoning. Perhaps these underlying abilities can be improved by practice on exercises similar to those in tests, as Binet suggested around 1900. If improved, more effective reading might be expected.

A fifth level of diagnosis related to reading improvement involves clinical analysis of personality traits and values. Administered and interpreted by a trained clinician, these analytical techniques may be influential in understanding an individual's reading performance. Such techniques as the figure drawing, incomplete sentences, Rorschach, Thematic Apperception Test (TAT), and other projective techniques may supplement, confirm, or contradict impressions gained from observation. The results of projective techniques may indicate the individual's need for psychotherapy preliminary to or concomitant with reading instruction.

A sixth level of diagnosis is the neurological examination of possible brain damage, neurological disorganization or malfunctioning, hemispheric dominance, and other pathological conditions. However, in view of "the present lack of definite correlations of brain pathology with inability to learn readily, to retain the meaning of what has been learned, and to recall that which is stored" (Cohn, 1962, p. 34), remediation must be based largely on observed behavior (Bateman, 1965, p. 168).

A seventh level is through introspective reports. On this level, the reader is invited to describe his process in reading selected articles. This aspect as yet has been barely explored. In the future, it may yield significant insights. While giving instruction, teachers may ask children how they managed to pronounce an unfamiliar word, or know the meaning of a word they had not been taught, or arrive at the meaning of a sentence or paragraph. They may be asked to explain a specific difficulty as they see it. Similar information can be obtained more precisely and systematically by trained research persons.

Teachers and clinicians each work on their level of competency and with reference to the complexity of the reading problem with which they are working. By using a team of specialists, the depth of diagnosis and treatment needed by an individual may be provided.

Contribution of research

There is practically no research on the diagnostic process *per se,* although a number of practical books on diagnosis and remediation have been recently published (Bond & Tinker, 1967; Hafner, 1967; Roswell & Natchez, 1964; Spache, 1963; Strang, 1964). Shorter theoretical treatments of the nature of diagnosis and remediation of learning difficulties appear in Barbara Bateman's (1965, 1966) articles. The *British Journal of Educational Psychology* devoted an entire issue to the diagnosis and treatment of learning difficulties (Curr & Gourlay, 1960; Dunham, 1960; Hillman & Snowdon, 1960; Moran, 1960; Roberts, 1960; M. D. Vernon, 1960).

There is extensive research dealing with the appraisal of reading performance, causes and correlates of reading development and difficulties, testing and other diagnostic techniques. There is also research on special problems of diagnosis of individuals of different ages and with various handicaps. Remediation, too, extends into a very broad field, including work with groups and with individual cases.

The research findings on each of these aspects are, for the most part, inconclusive. Generalizations and conclusions made in one study are often questioned or contradicted by another investigation. M. D. Vernon (1960) pointed out many of the prevalent difficulties in interpreting and using research on reading problems. For example, surveys show that poorer readers have less desirable qualities and live in more unfavorable environmental conditions than do better readers. But, such studies do not show how many and to what extent each of these qualities exists in poorer readers. Nor do investigations show whether lack of concentration, persistence, and emotional stability are the cause or the effect of difficulty in learning to read. Likewise, the superiority on tests of perception among first-grade good readers may be

> due, at least in part, to the reading (and writing) achievement of the better readers, which had taught them the necessity of distinguishing small details accurately. (M.D. Vernon, 1960, p. 151)

The reasons for the diversity and inadequacy of findings are quite obvious:

1] *Differences in population studied.* For example, in research on the relation of auditory discrimination to reading, the coefficients of correlation are usually higher with first- and second-grade children than with those in the intermediate grades. The relation is also more marked with disabled readers than with the general population.

2] *Different school conditions.* The situations as a whole are different and, therefore, the parts which are embedded in the whole are different.

3] *Variations in the experimental method.* For example, even when apparently the same method is used, there may be differences in the way it is administered and in the personality of the teachers. Teachers who are supposed to use a certain experimental method may slip in supplementary instruction in response to the pupil's needs. Thus, the results may be attributable to factors other than the experimental method.

4] *Contamination.* If the investigation is conducted within a given school or school system, other teachers learn about the experimental method and may use aspects of it in their classes.

5] *Hawthorne effect.* Teachers and pupils in the control group may be stimulated to achieve more than they normally would just by being in an experiment.

6] *Uncontrolled variables.* These influence the results in many experiments and make it impossible to say positively that the results were due to the experimental method *per se.*

7] *Different methods of collecting and treating the data.*

8] *Different philosophies.* The philosophy and convictions of the investigator may consciously or unconsciously influence his interpretation of the data and his conclusions.

In order to generalize from research studies, it would be necessary to repeat exactly the same procedure in various settings and to control all the variables that affect children's learning—and this is an obvious impossibility. Even under school or clinical conditions if correlations between various factors and reading achievement were much higher than those reported, it would be impossible to predict for individual cases. Moreover, prediction is impossible if the conditions that the individual will later face are unknown. More effective diagnosis and remediation would be accomplished if less time were spent on predictive studies and more time on perfecting methods of appraisal and on understanding the process by which an individual achieves reading competency.

What utility, then, do the findings of research have for diagnosis? Just this: they alert the diagnostician to a number of relationships that may possibly exist in a given group or in an individual. Instead of trying to predict from inadequate generalizations, the diagnostician can use the research findings with an expectation of different degrees of probability but not certainty. These findings serve as a background for understanding the many factors and patterns of factors which may be pertinent in a given case. If used in this way, the information presented here from many research studies can contribute to more effective diagnosis of reading achievement.

2. Correlates and causes of reading achievement and disability

As a basis for diagnosis, the teacher or clinician needs to know the characteristics and conditions that may be related to reading achievement or disability. These are factors to which the teacher should be alert in observing, interviewing, and testing.

Many research studies have been concerned with characteristics that distinguish good readers from poor readers of different ages. To review these studies thoroughly and arrive at some indication of their relative importance is a major task which was admirably accomplished in 1960 by M. D. Vernon. In this chapter, only information that seems to be most relevant to diagnosis and remediation is presented.

Most research deals with single factors, whereas the reading teacher and clinician are confronted with complex causation. There are many environmental, instructional, emotional, and motivational conditions which probably account for the large percentage of variance not attributed to the specific factors (Holmes, 1961). No support has been found for any single major cause for severe reading disability. Each diagnostician should keep in mind many possible explanations of a reading difficulty. He may examine first those which are most often associated with reading disability in individuals of different ages and backgrounds. Yet, it should be realized that frequencies of occurrence or even a high coefficient of correlation may not indicate the causative conditions in the case with whom he is working. That case may be one of the deviations from the central tendency.

The major explanations offered to account for reading disability are neuropathological disorders, mental retardation, sensory impairment, emotional disturbance, cultural deprivation, and deficient or ineffective instruction. Specialists concerned with the reading problem each tend to emphasize a major area. Those oriented toward medicine may consider neurological factors such as confused laterality, developmental lag, and other defects and disorders of the nervous system as mainly responsible for reading disability. Psychiatrists and clinical psychologists more often attribute reading disability to emotional conflicts and disturbed thinking which interfere with an individual's functioning. Using different methods of diagnosis, they are more likely to call attention to verbal intelligence and to neurological and emotional conditions. Reading specialists may emphasize visual-motor and perceptual-motor factors, reading skills, and learning theory. A team of physicians, neurologists, psychologists, and educators would give the deepest understanding of the multiple correlates and causes of reading difficulty.

A list of correlates may be derived from experience. The following overview of factors, believed to be related to reading difficulty, represents the opinions of authorities and third-grade teachers in the field (McMurray, 1963). Some of these are errors associated with children's reading performance:

Omits letters and words when copying material
Has trouble learning to spell a word by looking
    at it; he must write it
Forms printed words and letters poorly
Tends, when reading, to confuse words which start with
    the same letter but are otherwise different
Makes substitutions even for simple words
Reproduces correct letters but in the wrong order,
    i.e., *brid* for *bird*
Pronounces words incorrectly
Frequently fails to complete an assignment
Has speech problems at present, or in earlier grades

It is difficult to make the distinction between "causes" and errors, for an error which persists may be the cause of further reading difficulty.

Many other items reported in the McMurray (1963) study are social and emotional correlates:

Attention span shorter than the average

Difficulty in assuming responsibility and working
   independently
Tenseness, seldom relaxed
Daydreaming more than the average
Abnormal fears, worries, or problems at home
Unfavorable comparisons with siblings
Change of teachers
Unsatisfactory relationship with teachers
Unsatisfactory relationship with classmates
Change in handedness since coming to kindergarten
Lengthy illness prior to school entrance
Absence of more than twenty school days in a year

These items were thought to differentiate average from backward readers and to precipitate failure in reading.

In contrast with this opinion study is an example of an experimental type of investigation from which correlates may be derived. Backward readers were paired with average or good readers in the same school and matched according to their nonverbal reasoning score, social class, sex, or age (Lovell, Gray, & Oliver, 1964). In this investigation, the following tests were administered to 981 boys fourteen to fifteen years of age and to 872 girls of the same ages:

The WISC Vocabulary and Block Design test
Thurstone's Revision of the Gottschaldt Figures
Shapiro's Test of Rotation
Eight Bender-Gestalt designs plus three more difficult
   designs
The test of spatial orientation by Semmes, Weinstein,
   and others
A sentence-copying test
A dictation test

On these tests the backward readers made many errors, the boys about twice as many as the girls. Even at fourteen to fifteen years of age, the backward boys were deficient in visual perception; this was not true of the girls. The backward readers of both sexes made lower scores than the better readers on the WISC vocabulary test, but the mean vocabulary score for backward boys was not lower than that for backward girls. On the tests of dictation and sentence copying, a much higher number of errors were made by backward boys than by backward girls. The errors found most frequently among the backward children were: distortion of letters, incorrect letters, and addition of letters or words. Difficulties on tests involving spatial orientation and rotation did not differentiate the adolescent backward readers from the non-backward readers as they did with younger children previously studied.

Half of these backward readers had average or better non-verbal reasoning skills. This was true of younger children as well as of the adolescents.

From experiments of this kind, the diagnostician learns certain diagnostic signs to look for when he is working with a somewhat similar group. He would be alert to the greater number of errors made by the backward readers, the boys' greater difficulties in visual perception and on tests of dictation, and relatively low vocabulary scores for both boys and girls. He would also be alert to average and above-average reasoning skills which indicate that many backward children are "underestimated."

> Many backward pupils are capable of handling a wide range of ideas, assimilating much information, and achieving a satisfactory level of performance in many skills, providing reading and writing do not make too great demands on them. (Lovell, Gray, & Oliver, 1964, p. 279)

In the following pages, research on the more specific correlates—listening comprehension, oral language and speech, visual and auditory proficiency, perception and conceptualization—are first reviewed. Then, some of the more pervasive influences—environmental, neurological, intellectual, and emotional and personal characteristics—are reviewed. Although far from being exhaustive, this review of characteristics and conditions found to be related to retardation in reading should serve to alert the diagnostician to the factors that may be significant in the cases with whom he is working.

Listening comprehension (auding)

The relation between auding and reading achievement is close enough to warrant the attention of the diagnostician or teacher of reading (Witty & Sizemore, 1958, 1959). Listening and reading comprehension have about eighteen factors in common (Duker, 1964). Both are receptive acts; both require comprehension of words and sentence structure, critical thinking, and interpretation of meaning.

The coefficients of correlation between these two language arts are positive and significant, from .45 to .70 with a mean of .58. Holmes and Singer (1961) reported a correlation of .60 between speed of reading and listening comprehension as measured by the California Auding Test. The corresponding correlation with power of reading was .74. Those who are high in listening comprehension tend to be high in reading rate and comprehension. Training in one may improve proficiency in the other (Lundsteen, 1961).

The auditory avenue, in general, is preferred by the less able student and also by others when reading easy content; the visual avenue, by the more able student and for the more difficult material. Low auders tend to be especially deficient in word-recognition skills.

The rate of speaking is about 100 to 155 words per minute, the rate of listening 400 to 500 words per minute. The skillful listener takes advantage of this differential between the speed of speech and thought to relate or fix in mind what the speaker has said (Nichols & Stevens, 1957). Some individuals differ in their ability to perform on similar tests administered by listening and by reading, although group differences may not be evident (Westover, 1958). Listeners tend to be wordier, more repetitive, and more rambling than readers, whether reproducing by speaking or writing. But listeners make fewer omissions, reproduce the style of the original more faithfully, and recall a larger number of units. However, they are more likely than readers to distort the material they reproduce. This is true whether they reproduce the content by speaking or writing (Horowitz & Berkowitz, 1967).

Listening comprehension is one indication of reading potential. For this reason, a listening-comprehension test is often included in the diagnosis of reading difficulty. The purpose of such a test is to appraise comprehension of verbal material apart from the special skills required in reading. A relatively high listening-comprehension score is generally a favorable prognostic sign.

Many tests of listening comprehension have been developed. Duker (1966, p. 136) listed eighteen tests of listening comprehension. Several that are frequently referred to are:

The Sequential Test of Educational Progress: Listening
    (Educational Testing Service, 1956-63).
Diagnostic Reading Tests: Auditory Comprehension
    (Committee on Diagnostic Reading Tests, 1957-63).
*Brown-Carlsen Listening Comprehension Test: Evaluation
    and Adjustment Series* (Brown & Carlsen, 1953-55).
Test on critical listening—analysis and judgment of
    propaganda, described by Lundsteen (1963).

These tests must be used cautiously in the diagnosis of reading potential because of the wide range of reading abilities that exist and because of the variation in people's listening experiences. Some children growing up in an environment dominated by noise and quarreling have learned not to listen, whereas others may have had special instruction and practice in listening.

The diagnostic value of any test depends on the worker's knowledge of its relationship with other factors. Haberland (1959) found that the degree of correlation between certain listening tests and standardized tests depends a great deal on the general ability of the subjects. Moreover, the tests of listening —the Brown-Carlsen Listening Comprehension Test, Form AM; the Michigan State College Listening Test, Form III; and the Stephens College Test of Listening Comprehension, Form A—showed widely different coefficients of correlation with standardized intelligence, reading, and personality tests.

The Brown-Carlsen test showed the highest correlation with the linguistic sections of standardized tests, especially for women enrolled in regular freshman English classes. In contrast with the lack of agreement between the results of the listening tests and the academic ratings of students in regular English classes, a close agreement was found with students in the reading improvement course. This is another evidence of its possible value in predicting reading achievement.

Oral language and speech defects

Most children acquire reading ability through associating the printed word with their familiar spoken language. Any diagnostic procedure should include tests of oral vocabulary in isolation and in context, word fluency, word sense, and sentence length and structure. Holmes (1961) in his substrata-factor study found the linguistic factor to be one of the three major factors in reading speed and power.

Although the relationship between reading and speech development is readily acknowledged, its exact nature is still obscure. Theoretically, the relationship of defective speech to reading disability would be assumed. An individual hears the word as spoken by others differently from the way he speaks it. This difference is more pronounced if his articulation is not standard. When he sees the word in print, either of the two memories may be aroused. The speech difficulty may be one cause of reading difficulty or a result of an underlying cause. It may make an individual self-conscious, embarrassed, and negative toward all language situations including reading.

Experimental evidence of the relation between speech defects and reading proficiency is conflicting, although many investigations* show that this relation exists in various groups. It has been suggested that a history of speech defects may be asso-

---

* See, for example, Malmquist (1960, pp. 232-37).

ciated with retardation in reading, even when no definite relation between silent reading test scores and speech defects is
found in the older children. However, Malmquist (1960, p.
237) did not find a statistically positive relationship between
reading disabilities and speech defects even during pre-school
years.

Both speech and reading disorders, as Monroe (1946)
pointed out more than twenty years ago, may stem from some
common underlying conditions. These may be emotional disturbances, limited intelligence, physical impairments, environmental and educational deprivations, or immaturity resulting from
developmental lag. Such global involvement would affect to
some degree all the language skills.

Visual and auditory efficiency

All but a few exceptional children learn to read by associating the sound of familiar letters and words with their corresponding written symbol. Consequently, both visual and auditory acuity are a basis to success in beginning reading.

RELATION OF VISUAL FACTORS TO READING

Over the years various aspects of visual efficiency, important in reading diagnosis, have been studied and reviewed
by Eames. In 1959 Eames published a detailed review of
studies of eye handicaps to reading, comparative eye conditions among reading failures and unselected pupils, classroom
help for children with eye difficulties, and eye-screening tests.

To see clearly, eyes must work well together, diverge and
converge at will, and integrate two images into one. To achieve
this, numerous experiences of integrating sensations are necessary. Normal vision is an important precondition of maximum
reading comfort and efficiency; it is basic to perception. Proba-

bly far too many children have been handicapped in beginning reading because of undetected visual impairments, most frequently muscular imbalance and problems of convergence.

In a number of studies, specific visual defects have been reported as negatively related to successful reading: farsightedness, astigmatism, binocular incoordination, fusion difficulties (Rosen, 1965). The myopes tend to be better readers than those who are farsighted. Farsightedness has been reported in 43 per cent of retarded readers, as compared with 12 per cent of unselected children. One type of refractive error, anisometropia, in which the images of the two eyes may be distorted in various ways, may be an impediment to reading achievement. Eames (1964) found that correction of anisometropia helped a number of pupils about nine years of age achieve more closely to their potential ability.

Estimates of the incidence of visual defects among retarded readers vary greatly. Helen M. Robinson (1953) found that more than half of the reading cases at the University of Chicago reading clinics had vision problems which either needed correction or had already been corrected. The incidence of visual problems is high enough to recommend that a visual screening test be given to all cases of reading disability.

The results of research on the relation of specific visual defects to reading disability are contradictory. One reason why it is difficult to get clear-cut evidence of the relation of visual defects to reading is that some children with certain visual defects can be successful in reading, while others in whom visual defects are barely recognized may be severely retarded in reading. The effects of slight defects of visual fusion and ocular-motor coordination in the development of reading ability are still obscure. The relationship seems to be more pronounced in kindergarten children than in older children who may have learned to compensate for their visual defects.

In 1959 Huelsman reviewed nine studies published since 1950 related to outline form perception, the use of the tachistoscope, and general visual achievement. One study showed a significant relationship between perceptual ability and school achievement with primary-age children; two other studies did not find this relationship at the fourth- and fifth-grade levels; a fourth study considered the learning disability to be characteristic of the immature child who "retains infantile habits of perception and visual-motor performance" (Huelsman, 1959, p. 3).

The value of tachistoscopic training is likewise controversial. In Huelsman's (1959) review, one study found that improvement in reading rate and comprehension paralleled tachistoscopic training. Another study reported that the group taught without the tachistoscope exceeded the group in which the tachistoscopic training was used in reading rate, there was no difference in fixations, regressions, span of recognition, or duration of fixations.

Studies of the relationships between reading achievement and various measures of vision were also inconclusive. Three of the four investigations reviewed by Huelsman failed to find conclusive statistically reliable differences in reading achievement between visual-defect groups and groups with normal vision. A case study and developmental approach in which combinations of visual defects are studied would be "more analytical and definitive in its conclusions" (Huelsman, 1959, p. 6).

Refractive errors apparently are not related to intelligence. When reading achievement is parceled out, the correlation between the intelligence-test scores and refractive errors tend to approach zero (Young, 1963).

Lack of ocular efficiency and visual-motor capacity may distort results on tests of perception in which it is generally assumed that the subjects have normal visual acuity. Poor visual acuity may be a cause of reading disability, insofar as beginning readers may not be able to grasp the symbolic significance of letters because they cannot obtain a clear visual impression of them. "A poor performance on visual-motor tasks does not necessarily indicate impairment in either the visual or the motor system but rather may indicate a central dysfunction which is reflected in the motor response" (Leton, 1962, p. 407).

Good readers tend to have good fusion, though some are "one-eyed" readers. Stereopsis does not seem to be directly related to reading proficiency. Both esophoria (tendency of the eyes to turn inward) and exophoria (tendency of the eyes to turn outward) at both near- and far-point fusion are associated with poor reading scores. "Generally myopia with no lateral imbalance and good fusion is associated with good readers, while hyperopia, lateral imbalance, overconvergence, and fusion problems are associated with poor readers" (Spache & Tillman, 1962, p. 102).

The search for a single factor causing reading disability is seldom valid. Other factors usually are operating along with visual difficulties. Visual factors may be directly related, contributory, or coincidental to the reading disability. The relationship of patterns of visual defects to visual perception and to specific reading disabilities should be studied further.

DIAGNOSIS AND PREVENTION OF VISUAL DEFECTS

Prevention and remediation require initial identification of visual problems by the teacher, accurate visual screening, referral if necessary to a professionally competent person, follow-up of the eye examination to see that recommended correction and treatment of muscular imbalance and convergence defects are provided, and necessary adjustments made in the classroom.

The teacher observes how the child uses his eyes in a given situation. Can he shift with ease from far to near and from near to far vision? Is there good teaming and coordination between the two eyes? How well does he coordinate eye and hand in manipulating eating utensils, pencils, toys? Visual guidance for manual dexterity and ocular-motor patterns set the stage for perception. Eye-movement skills reduce the need for motor aspects, e.g. moving the head while reading. Total developmental factors—the total action system of the child—are involved in the organization of his visual abilities as they relate to reading.

Periodic visual examination during school years should include appraisal of the developmental factors that contribute to visual efficiency. Infants' eyes need the stimulation of contrast between light and dark. They need experience in looking at targets with patterns. Two-year-olds need to move freely and develop both sides of the body. They learn through their play activities, and vision becomes increasingly dominant in learning. During pre-school years, systematic examinations and supervision are necessary to identify potential difficulties in learning to read.

The age of seven seems to be a crucial period requiring special supervision. The child may develop stabismus—lack of coordination of the two eyes—and over-organization at near-point distance. After a time, he may become a myope. Convergence exercises may be given, either at home or by an orthoptic technician, to improve this particular ability. Improvement in reading accompanying these exercises may be due to improved concentration rather than to the exercises themselves.

Visual screening should include a binocular reading test, a hand-eye coordination test, and teacher observation. If teachers' observations are improved by training and the use of a check list as a guide, they compare favorably with screening tests. An efficient vision-screening instrument is the School Vision Tester, a modification of the Bausch and Lomb Orthorater.

The opthalmograph or eye-movement camera has been suggested as an instrument for measuring visual efficiency. A skilled technician can detect gross changes in vergence during reading, lack of relationship between vergence and accommodation as seen in regressive movements, and lack of vertical control (Waldstreicher, 1966). However, there is insufficient evidence to show that the eye-movement camera has much diagnostic value for reading except to determine the number and length of fixations, and these have little significance without reference to the reader's purpose and the kind of material. The better students may regress more often so that they can read more carefully. Moreover, a mere movement of the eyes does not mean that the reader is comprehending the passage. The eye-movement record is, as pointed out by Gruber (1962), in general, unreliable in assessing binocular coordination, muscle imbalance, and lack of fusional ability. It is not a substitute for a competent examination by an eye specialist.

Attention should be given to developing more efficient and effective instruments and techniques for detecting visual impairments and to interpreting and applying the results to reading problems.

Auditory factors in reading diagnosis

Although research on the relationship between auditory functions and success in reading is conflicting, there is evidence enough to recommend including tests of auditory acuity in the diagnosis of reading problems. Hard-of-hearing and deaf children are generally retarded in reading skills and are especially deficient in phonic skills, oral reading, and spelling.

Actual hearing loss and fluctuations in auditory acuity may impede reading progress because they make it difficult for children to learn sound-letter associations. Audiograms detect difficulties in learning by the phonic method. Spache (1963, pp. 113-14) noted that a large proportion of the consonant sounds such as *p, s, t, b, k, v, c, fl, ch, th* are found among the high tones. Inability to hear low tones clearly may make it difficult for the child to identify vowel sounds linked with *r, g, b, h,* and their blends. Combinations of both low and high tone losses leave the pupil extremely handicapped except for the strong vowels *a* and *o.* Audiometric tests for acuity are widely recognized and accepted. An indefinite number of reading problems may be prevented by obtaining audiograms for all children during the first year and at least every third year thereafter.

To give the child with impaired hearing practice in discriminating various phonetic elements in word combinations, Haspiel and Bloomer (1961) developed the Maxium Auditory Perception word list (MAP) consisting of

monosyllabic words containing the various English phonetic elements permuted and combined with each other in a sequential order. The sequence of sounds is based upon their discriminability from each other, their time of development, and their frequency of occurrence. The MAP word list has application in auditory training, diagnosis of discrimination ability, and remedial reading. (1961, p. 163)

Other physical factors may be of greater importance as causes of reading failure than has generally been recognized (Richardson, 1958; Stott, 1959).

Perception and conceptualization

Word perception differs from sensory impressions in that meaning has been added—meaning derived from previous first-hand experiences and reading. The beginning reading process usually follows this sequence: Visual impressions and perceptions + auditory associations → pronunciation → recognition of meaning → conceptualization. Concepts are developed from perceptions. This process requires the ability to recall perceptions and to manipulate them in the mind.

There may be three levels of perceptual ability: *1*] an early level of perceptual discrimination in which the child can distinguish different objects, *2*] a later level of perceptual analysis in which he recognizes parts from the whole configuration, *3*] a still later level of perceptual synthesis which involves the ability to combine parts into a whole configuration.

Perception depends upon cognitive as well as upon sensory processes. The intellectual abilities necessary for beginning reading are different from those required for the more complex comprehension of reading material. In the first grade, the Quantitative, Perception, and Space sub-tests of the Primary Mental Abilities Test showed the highest correlation with reading scores. In the fourth grade, the Verbal Meaning, Reasoning, and Number sub-tests were the best predictors of reading achievement (Reed, 1958). This relationship between perception, mental ability, and reading achievement may be one explanation of the difficulty that the less able children begin to have in the fourth and higher grades.

Emotional and motivational factors also influence perception. Frustration caused by unnecessary parental inhibitions and punishment of exploratory behavior that results in the suppression of curiosity often contribute to difficulties in beginning reading (Walters, Van Loan, & Crofts, 1961). Retarded readers appear to have difficulties in decision-making and often lack the motivation to perform at optimum efficiency. "Need, too, is a determiner of perception" (Alexander & Money, 1965, p. 981). Except in the early stages, the problem does not seem to be one of perception *per se*, but rather the translation of perceptions into concepts that can be used in reading and related language functions.

RELATION OF PERCEPTION TO READING ABILITY

It seems clear that perceptual skills play an important role in reading achievement in the beginning stages, perhaps a more important role than emotional factors or mental ability.

In general, average and superior readers tend to perform better than retarded readers on tests of closure, perceptual differentiation, and measures of lag in perceptual maturation. The below-average readers tend to be relatively weak in perceptual discrimination and symbolic learning and slower in reaction time to a multiple-choice task. The younger superior readers resemble older average pupils in visual-motor development. Gifted children seem to be accelerated in this ability and, by ages eight or nine, they may have developed conceptual and other abilities that enhance their reading development (Chang & Chang, 1967).

Since perception involves large portions of the cortical tissue, "no longer are we *surprised* to find perceptual disturbances accompanying problems of minimal brain damage, certain emotional problems, and certain conditions of inadequate learning experiences" (Kephart, 1963, p. 30).

A longitudinal study by Silver and Hagin (1963) employed a battery of tests to assess aspects of perception, neurological status, educational achievement, psychiatric and social adjustment, and cognitive function of twenty-five children in the Bellevue Mental Hygiene Clinic. A follow-up study twelve years later showed some deficits to be more persistent than others. Among these were visual perception errors in angulation, displacement, and tactile perception. The children with signs of neurological disorganization tended to have the greater perceptual deficits as adults. Errors in left-right discrimination so prominent in childhood were significantly decreased. The more adequate adult readers were those who had been less severely retarded in reading as children. As children they had made a higher proportion of verticalization and rotation errors in the Bender-Gestalt, but significantly fewer figure-background errors in perception (Silver & Hagin, 1963). It seems evident that visual and auditory perception and discrimination are not unitary factors; each consists of a number of specific abilities and is related to other factors such as factual perception, laterality, body-image, and visual-space perceptions. Body-image problems have not been clearly demonstrated in the Benton and Kemble Right-Left Discrimination Battery (1959) and localization tests and similar approaches have likewise yielded uncertain results. Children "show marked subjective reaction to the orientational dilemma" (Rabinovitch, 1962, p. 77). Perceptions of objects in space seem to require experience early in life which later experience does little to modify (Epstein, 1964).

Many studies have reported a closer relationship between perception and reading achievement in the first grade than in later years. However, the decreased relationship between perceptual-motor problems and reading ability on the older age level may be misleading because maturation, training, and compensations have obscured the role they actually played in reading achievement.

Since perceptual skills play an important role in reading

achievement during the beginning stages of reading, reading teachers and psychologists should assess perceptual abilities of children earlier and more thoroughly and differentially than they do at present. They should include, as part of their diagnostic procedure for kindergarten children and children entering the first grade, tests of visual and auditory perception, discrimination, memory, and integration. They should also help teachers to identify children's strengths and weaknesses in each of these aspects of perception as they carry on their familiar readiness program. While focusing attention on visual and auditory perception, both specialists and teachers can begin to develop concepts which depend upon and thus help to organize specific perceptions.

Having identified children's perceptual patterns, the specialist and teacher may adapt the curriculum to children with special perceptual abilities or deficiencies. Such adaptation would involve using their preferred mode of learning and also giving practice in the aspects of perception in which they are deficient.

Three conditions conducive to learning in the area of perception are generally not sufficiently recognized. The first is the importance of satisfaction in learning. When a learning task is relatively difficult, the individual often needs incentives in addition to those inherent in successful accomplishment. Unless highly motivated, retarded readers are not attentive, especially to auditory stimuli. It may be that some of them have been subjected to so much noise and dissension in their environment that they tend to tune out auditory stimuli in school and learn to ignore them.

The second condition of effective learning involves the relation of intelligence to reading; intelligence is involved in every aspect of reading. Exercises that improve reasoning and judgment would seem to be more effective in remedial reading classes than drill on sound-letter associations alone. For example, in teaching the initial consonants, exercises that give practice in the form of a riddle—"fox - box, which is an animal?"— are more effective than just drill on initial consonant sounds.

The third condition is involvement of the individual in the perceptual process. It is encouraging that once the general nature of symbolic learning is understood, the retarded readers can generalize the principles to facilitate learning in somewhat similar situations. In one study (Walters & Doan, 1962), the retarded readers improved on the second trial in both visual and auditory tasks. Moreover, pre-training on the visual task helped them to respond more quickly to the auditory symbol. Their lack of perceptual ability seemed not to be primarily a deficit in their ability to form associations, but rather inability to attend to stimuli.

Money (1962, p. 29) warns of the danger of taking valid hypotheses and principles of development and applying them "prematurely and untested, as principles of training and treatment, with unjustified reliance on disproved assumptions concerning . . . transfer of training."

THE PROCESS OF VISUAL PERCEPTION

Visual perception is the process by which the visual form of words is recognized, small details distinguished, and the printed symbol associated with an object or event. From about seven years of age, the cognitive or intellectual development becomes increasingly prominent. The process of visual perception has been described by Goins (1958), Kass (1966), and M.D. Vernon (1960) as follows: The wholeness of a word, phrase, or sentence and its parts must be held in mind simultaneously. The individual must pay attention to the configuration of the word as a pattern having a sequence of letters and distinguishing characteristics. This ability requires strength of closure and the ability to relate interior details to the whole pattern of the word. Perceiving only the general form of a word may cause as much difficulty in reading as does over-attention to detail and word analysis.

Research with pre-school children (Gibson, Gibson, Pick, & Osser, 1962) has described children's ability to discriminate graphic symbols and letter-like forms when they are oriented differently in space. Certain types of errors were eliminated early. For example, four-year-old children can overcome errors such as confusing an *o* and a *c*. Since they easily read pictures upside down, they have difficulty in discriminating *u* from *n* and *d* from *b* which are similar except for their orientation in space. Such reversals, Gibson, Gibson, Pick, and Osser (1962) found, were usually overcome by the age of eight. Children with severe reading disability had difficulty in reproducing symbols presented visually, in blending parts into wholes, and in comparing detailed figures (Kass, 1966).

Many teachers are surprised when children recognize long words more easily than short words like *there, then, when.* This is explainable. The short words are about equal in length, similar in configuration, and have no characteristic features which give clues to their recognition. Furthermore, these structural words are abstract in nature; they represent spatial, temporal, and causal relations and have no object or action referents.

Eye-movement studies have shown that meaningful words can be comprehended as easily as single letters and that rapid reading is achieved by clue reduction, i.e. by reconstructing the meaning from a few distinguishing features. Psychological recognition takes place primarily during the fixations or pauses.

Recognition of printed words, unlike recognition of objects, demands that children note small changes in form, position, or directional orientation. As pointed out by Alexander and Money (1965), children should make the generalization that such small changes in form and directional orientation of letters alter their symbolic or semantic meaning. For example, *p* turned around in different directions becomes *g, d,* or *b*. An *e* without the little cross lines becomes a *c*. If the serial position of letters in *was* is reversed, it becomes *saw.*

On the other hand, children also discover another generalization: that some inconstancy of form is permissible. For example, a letter will have the same symbolic value whether it be written in capital or lower-case form, in print, manuscript, or script writing.

Children can gain this basic information and understanding by exercises in which they have to distinguish the letter or word form that is different from three others. After they have indicated their choice, the teacher should ask them to tell and show how they made this differentiation.

In the first grade, children's ability to perceive and distinguish between similar letters was found to be more closely related to reading ability than was visual perception of geometric forms, shapes, or pictures (Malmquist, 1960; Goins, 1958).

VISUAL IMAGERY

Visual imagery, which is ability to create mental images with photographic clarity—to "see it in the mind's eye"—has also been called "visual memory," "mental imagery," "imagery," "visual memory," "inner perception," "re-perception," "visualization." Some kind of visual memory is obviously essential in learning to read (Pennema, 1959). There is some evidence that children who consistently use imagery in their reading have more vivid and meaningful experiences. Radaker (1962) found this to be true with fourth-grade children who were given a history assignment containing vivid descriptions. The children were asked *1*] to describe in writing the mental picture created, *2*] to write an original story that involved the characters and scenes, and *3*] to illustrate their stories. To measure visual imagery, Radaker constructed a visual-imagery index, a memory-for-objects test, and a memory-for-words test. He also administered the Stanford Binet memory-for-designs test and the Graham and Kendall memory of sixteen small objects. The group that was given practice in visual imagery consistently outgained the control group.

AUDITORY PERCEPTION

Auditory perception, discrimination, and memory are also essential to progress in word recognition according to well-known authorities (Wepman, 1960; Durrell & Murphy, 1953; Caffrey & Michael, 1955). Undoubtedly there are many retarded readers who are deficient in auditory skill.

Wepman (1962) found that 27 per cent of 80 first-grade children with inadequate auditory discrimination had reading scores below the level of children with adequate auditory discrimination. Deutsch (1964) proposed as a minimum level of auditory discrimination requisite for the acquisiton of verbal skills not more than seven to eight errors on the Wepman Auditory Discrimination Test. Once that minimum level is reached, auditory discrimination may no longer be highly correlated with language abilities. Walters and Kosowski (1963) suggested that retarded readers, unless highly motivated, may pay less attention to reading because auditory discrimination requires so much effort on their part.

Even investigations employing similar techniques but with different populations of elementary and secondary students report different results, ranging from no relationship to substantial positive coefficients of correlation. Several general conclusions may be drawn from earlier studies:

1] Auditory discrimination appears to be significantly related to, though not necessarily a cause of, reading achievement in the lower grades, while less so in the upper grades.

2] The highest correlations with reading achievement were those using auditory discrimination tests that measured abilities similar to those the children had been taught.

3] Unsuccessful readers usually showed marked deficiencies in auditory discrimination.

4] Girls were superior to boys in rhyming, auditory discrimination, and use of context and auditory clues; boys apparently learned auditory discrimination skills less readily and took longer to master the reading process.

The marked discrepancy in results of different investigations is illustrated by two more recent studies, both with first-grade children. Both studies used the word-recognition and paragraph-reading sub-tests of the Gates Primary Reading Test as a measure of reading achievement but used different tests of intelligence and auditory discrimination. The first was a longitudinal study by Bertha B. Thompson (1963) who compared four groups:

24 from the upper end of the distribution in reading
24 who placed at the lower end
24 whose reading age most exceeded their mental age
24 whose mental age exceeded their reading age.

Thompson eliminated the factor of auditory acuity by giving individual pure-tone audiometer tests to those who failed the preliminary screening tests. The tests of auditory discrimination used were: Wepman Auditory Discrimination Test (Wepman, 1958); Boston University Speech Sound Discrimination Picture Test; Auditory Discrimination orientation, a sub-test of the SRA Reading Achievement Series (Lefever & Hashind, 1954-64). Intelligence was measured by the Wechsler Intelligence Scale for Children (Wechsler, 1949). Thompson found that auditory discrimination and intelligence are highly correlated with success in primary reading at the beginning of the first year. Although children grow in auditory discrimination during the first two years, it is not fully developed in all children, especially in poor readers, during that period. If a child entering first grade is high in auditory discrimination, he has a good chance of becoming a good reader, other things being equal. On the WISC, the mean-performance-scale I.Q. of these poor readers was significantly higher than their verbal-scale I.Q.. The only significant difference in sub-tests between the good and the poor readers was the Coding Test which might have been affected by lack of motor coordination in using a pencil.

A still more recent study of the relationship between auditory discrimination and reading achievement, reported by Dykstra (1966), obtained very different results. In Dykstra's group of 632 first-grade children from all socio-economic levels, the mean intelligence, as measured by the Lorge-Thorndike Intelli-

gence Tests, Form B, Level One, was 102. Reading ability at
the end of the first grade was measured by the word-recognition
and paragraph-reading sub-tests from the Gates Primary Reading Test. The seven tests used to measure auditory discrimination were selected from published reading-readiness tests. They
covered the following aspects of auditory discrimination:

  Rhyming test from the Gates Reading Readiness Test
    (Gates, 1939-42)
  Making auditory discriminations and using context and
    auditory clues from the Harrison-Stroud Reading
    Readiness Profiles (Harrison & Stroud, 1949-56)
  Auditory discrimination of beginning sounds and ending
    sounds from the Murphy-Durrell Diagnostic Reading
    Readiness Test (Murphy & Durrell, 1947-49)
  Discrimination of correct pronunciation and auditory
    blending, Reading Aptitude Tests (Monroe, 1935)

Although all seven tests purported to measure auditory discrimination, the intercorrelations among them were consistently
low, mostly below .40. For example, the correlation between
the Murphy-Durrell sub-test of Discrimination of Beginning
Sounds and the Harrison-Stroud auditory discrimination test
was only .30, yet they purport to measure essentially the same
skills. The Harrison-Stroud ranked second only to the intelligence test in its contribution to the prediction of reading achievement, while the Murphy-Durrell failed to contribute significantly
to any predictive multiple regression equation.

The Lorge-Thorndike Intelligence Test was consistently
one of the best predictors of reading achievement; intelligence
plus five of the auditory discrimination tasks was the best combination of the tests used. They were significantly related to
both paragraph reading and word recognition. The relation between auditory discrimination and age was negligible, from .003
to .095; the older first graders were no better in auditory discrimination than the younger readers. On the basis of this study,
Dykstra saw "no justification for spending more than twenty to
thirty minutes testing auditory discrimination ability of first-
grade pupils" (1966, p. 32).

The differences in the results of these studies, one advocating and the other questioning the value of a diagnostic battery of tests of auditory discrimination, are obviously at least partly due to the differences in the sample, in the tests used, and in the statistical treatment of the data. But, in view of the generally positive relationship, auditory discrimination should not be neglected in a diagnostic program. Administered early to all children, a short test of auditory discrimination would detect certain children who need special help in developing this ability. Administered to older retarded readers, it would help to identify one factor that might be hampering their progress in reading.

Auditory disorders may be: *1*] essentially developmental, *2*] the result of inadequate instruction and faulty learning, or *3*] the result of impairment or dysfunction of the auditory apparatus. Diagnosis should be concerned with home and family conditions that may facilitate or inhibit the development of auditory skills. Children from verbally-oriented homes, where conversation occurs frequently and members of the family use an elaborated language pattern when speaking to children, have a marked advantage in beginning reading over children from environments in which there is only rudimentary verbal communication.

The Wepman Test of Auditory Discrimination, which takes only a few minutes to administer, and the teacher's day-by-day observation probably would yield enough valuable diagnostic information on auditory discrimination to the first-grade teacher of reading.

Other tests of auditory discrimination give information on various aspects. Pronovost and Dumbleton(1953)developed a picture-type sound-discrimination test in which the child is asked to point to the picture pair named by the examiner, i.e. "Show me the bear-pear," "Show me the comb-comb."

Two auditory items are included on the Primary Form of the Reading Aptitude Test (Monroe, 1935). The test presents a picture, e.g. a boat with three numbers under it; the child identifies the right name for the picture as the examiner says, "This is a beef" (pointing to No. 1), "This is a boat," (pointing to No. 2), "This is a boot" (pointing to No. 3). "Which one was right?"

Another auditory skill is ability to respond to the meaning of spoken sentences, as in the sentence test of the Metropolitan Readiness tests. The examiner says a sentence describing a picture which the child then identifies.

Auditory memory is tested by the digit span on the Stanford-Binet and the WISC. Other kinds of responses to auditory stimuli presented are production of taped patterns and recall of a story told to the subjects.

When deficiencies in auditory perception, discrimination, and memory are detected, systematic training in auditory discrimination of sounds, letters, words, and sentences can be given in the classroom to the group who have this special difficulty. First a noise may be made behind a screen, and the children guess what the noise was. Learning to identify the beginning consonant in words also can be fun if presented as a game in which children discriminate between pairs of words given orally by the teacher: *cat, hat; can, man;* which has the *c* sound? Or riddles may be used: *cow, bow;* which is an animal? Or sentences with one word omitted except for the initial sound: Jack gave Jane a piece of c____. Or directions given orally which the child carries out: Come here and get a piece of candy. Readiness workbooks and teacher guides to basal readers are full of exercises that the teacher may use with children who need to develop auditory discrimination abilities. It is equally important that children who test high in auditory discrimination be introduced to the next stages in word study and reading appropriate for them.

INTEGRATION OF AUDITORY AND VISUAL IMPRESSIONS

Although a few children may acquire reading ability as a visual skill, "others do so through a combined phonetic-phonemic-visual integration" (Wepman, 1962, p. 183). The nervous system integrates the impressions brought in by the five senses. One possible cause of reading disability could be "a primary inadequacy in the ability to integrate auditory and visual stimuli" (Birch & Belmont, 1964, p. 852). Auditory-visual integration, being basic to phonics, might be expected to occur more commonly in normal readers than in a group of children retarded in reading.

To test this hypothesis, Birch and Belmont (1964) devised an ingenious test in which the subjects had to identify a visual-dot pattern that corresponded to a rhythmic-auditory pattern. They found that "a low score on the auditory-visual pattern test not only served to distinguish retarded readers from normal readers, but within each of those groups tended to identify those with lower reading scores" (1964, p. 856). Although normal readers did achieve significantly higher mean I.Q.'s than the retarded readers, they were higher in auditory-visual integration than were the retarded readers as a group even when I.Q. was held constant. Therefore, the relation of auditory-visual test performance to reading cannot be attributed to I.Q. differences. It would seem that special difficulties in integration are faced by retarded readers. In its more complex form, auditory-visual integration may be one of the processes that underlie the I.Q.; the more intelligent children may be those who are able to integrate their multi-modal sensory impressions.

Difficulties in auditory-visual integration could occur if either sensory avenue were impaired. Therefore, the diagnostic procedure might follow this sequence: *1*] tests of auditory and visual efficiency;   *2*] tests of auditory and visual perception, discrimination, and memory such as the Digit Span sub-test of the WISC;   *3*] test of auditory-visual integration.

In another experiment, Birch and Belmont (1965) likewise found high correlations between auditory-visual integration and reading skills for young children. They reported that growth in auditory-visual integration was most rapid between kindergarten and second grades, between the ages of six and seven, and reached a peak by the fifth grade. The correlations between auditory-visual integration decreased with age.

In contrast, the correlation between I.Q. and reading ability rose with age. Auditory-visual integration and intelligence are associated, but not synonymous. The perceptual factors are prerequisite to beginning reading, but general intelligence facilitates the acquisition of more mature reading ability. In the later stages of reading development, the higher correlation between reading achievement and I.Q. suggests that "reading skills have become linked with interests, experience, and conceptual factors" (Birch & Belmont, 1965, p. 302).

SIGNIFICANCE FOR DIAGNOSIS OF RESEARCH ON VISUAL AND AUDITORY PERCEPTION

The results of research on visual-auditory perception suggest the following procedures for diagnostic study and remediation:

1] Results of tests of visual and auditory perception may be distorted by basic physical defects. Therefore, impairment of vision and hearing should be tested prior to giving tests of visual and auditory perception.

2] In testing the related aspects of perception, various elements must be recognized: discrimination, memory, integration of visual and auditory, and ability to communicate one's perception.

3] Since the relation between perceptual factors and reading readiness and achievement is much higher in the pre-school, kindergarten, and beginning years than later, deficiencies in perception should be detected early.

4] Differential diagnosis is much more useful than a total score or level, for it indicates specific strengths and deficiencies.

5] Although simple auditory and visual perceptual tasks do

not have a high correlation with intelligence as measured, the more complex aspects of perception that may underlie intelligence should be recognized.

6] Exercises similar to those used in diagnosis may be developed to give practice and instruction on aspects in which the individual is deficient (Farnham-Diggory, 1967). Many readiness exercises that teachers are now using are effective in overcoming perceptual weakness in pre-school and first-grade pupils. By observing the responses of children to these exercises, teachers may continuously appraise their diagnostic methods and obtain information concerning perception which they can use immediately in remediation.

Goins (1958) did not find that tachistoscopic training in Gestalt perception improved the general visual perceptual ability of first-grade children.

A developmental or maturational approach was suggested by Hagin, Silver, and Hersh (1965) to increasing children's perceptual ability. In this approach, training would begin at the individual's lowest level of functioning and follow a sequence of perceptual maturation from the most elementary to the more complex. When the child has achieved mastery of relatively simple forms, he would progress to asymmetric forms, to matrix-like forms, to complex forms. To confront him with too difficult tasks in the beginning would undermine his confidence in his ability to learn and in himself as a person. As a measure of mastery, Hagin, Silver, and Hersh (1965) suggested the three-by-three rule: three correct performances for three consecutive weeks. The children develop accuracy through visual matching, copying, and recall. Verbal instruction and any aid such as color clues are used to increase learning. Such training may stimulate maturation essential for reading. Although perceptual defects persist tenaciously in the retarded reader, perception has been modified by training and this improvement has been reflected in better reading (Hagin, Silver, & Hersh, 1965, p. 370).

Environmental factors

For the most part, researchers have directed their attention to the psychic structure, the neurological and psychological substrata, and the genetic and developmental history of the child himself as the explanation of his reading disability. An ecological view directs attention to environmental conditions that may give rise to or intensify reading difficulties. The fault lies not only in the child but also in the environment to which he reacts and which responds to his behavior (Rhodes, 1967). Improvement in reading involves not only learning theory but also personal relations, intra-group relations, home conditions, and other elements interwoven with reading instruction. Therefore, diagnosis should include an analysis of the situation as well as of the individual and be concerned with the interaction with his environment.

Following such a diagnosis would be an effort to change the situation instead of the child. Instead of removing the child from the setting of the difficulty by putting him in a special class, a reading teacher would work with the child in a regular class, team teaching with his subject teacher. If possible, the reading teacher would work with the family unit, helping the parents to perceive the child in a more favorable light.

SOCIO-ECONOMIC STATUS

One of the environmental factors that has been extensively studied in sociological research and recently in connection with reading achievement is the socio-economic status of the family. A study of the total third-grade population of nine classrooms in three schools (Hill & Giammatteo, 1963) showed a relationship between socio-economic status and reading comprehension and vocabulary. When Lovell and Woolsey (1964) studied reading achievement with reference to socio-economic status as based on occupational classification, they found a higher frequency of reading backwardness in the lower socio-

economic group. Harris (1961) reported that a higher proportion of disturbed boys with learning problems were from lower
socio-economic classes, but there were also other aspects of
their life which were a deterrent to school achievement. According to Sutton (1964), readiness for reading at the kindergarten
level was associated with a relatively high socio-economic level
and parents engaged in the professions. Another study
(Malmquist, 1961) found only 2 children out of 48 from the
highest social class were poor readers. However, Durkin
(1963) reported that more than half of the parents of early
readers in the second study were foreign born and came from
the "blue-collar" class. Speasl and Herrington (1965) found
no difference in reading achievement based upon standardized
tests of sixth-grade children in high, medium, and low socio-
economic levels, but they did find differences in reading readiness among the three socio-economic levels.

Diagnostic information should always be interpreted in the
light of environmental conditions that may modify it. Certain
conditions may be interfering with the progress of the potential
poor readers in any socio-economic status group, and these conditions should be taken into consideration in the remedial program.

MOBILITY

How frequently is mobility of the family related to the
child's school achievement? The change of teachers and teaching method as well as the social adjustment with peers neces-
sitated by a change of school would seem to be detrimental
to reading achievement. However, in Bollenbacher's (1962)
study involving 95 per cent of the sixth-grade pupils in the
public schools of Cincinnati, mobility did not seem to be associated with pupils' achievement in arithmetic and reading, although the children who moved frequently tended to have lower
I.Q.'s . Evans' (1966) study of children whose fathers were in
the armed services showed no significant difference in the I.Q.'s

between those who had moved frequently and those who had not moved. The mobile group even showed a small superiority in reading and science.

There seems to be no research evidence that mobility *per se* is associated with failure in reading. In individual cases of retarded readers who have moved frequently, other factors may be more influential than mobility.

EDUCATION OF PARENTS

Although the influence of social class and mobility *per se* on children's reading achievement has not been verified, a related factor—the influence of the parents' education and interest in reading—has been more clearly established. In Malmquist's (1960) experiment, only 5 poor readers out of 52 had fathers whose education was above elementary level, and only 2 had mothers who had gone beyond elementary school. The relation between the mother's education and the child's reading ability was found to be strongly significant. Other investigations warrant the practice of obtaining information on the education of parents in diagnostic studies.

ATTITUDES OF PARENTS

The influence of parents' attitudes is much more subtle and difficult to ascertain. Using the Parental Attitude Research Instrument (PARI) (Bell & Schaefer, 1957), and MacDonald (1963) found a marked difference in parental attitudes toward unsuccessful readers in the University Children's Clinic and also in the attitudes of parents of unsuccessful and successful readers in the public schools who came to the Child Guidance Clinic. The University Clinic mothers were inclined to be less strict, and less likely to suppress their children's curiosity about sex than the public school mothers of both unsuccessful and successful readers. The fathers of children attending the clinic were inclined to be less likely than the public school fathers to suppress their children's aggression and curiosity about sex. They were also less likely to feel that children should never learn things outside the home which would make them doubt their parents' ideas. The lack of differentiation in parental attitude toward successful and unsuccessful readers (assuming a certain reliability and validity for the PARI) suggests that it is not the expressed attitude of parents that is related to success in reading, but the way in which the children perceive it.

HOME CONDITIONS

Many home factors have been suggested as related to reading achievement: general emotional atmosphere, number of books in the home, the child's position in the family, interfamily relationships. Although it is generally believed that home conditions do exert a strong influence on the development of a child's reading ability, the correlations reported are, for the most part, low. Undoubtedly, various combinations of home conditions do affect the child's reading as a part of his total adjustment.

Sutton (1964) found that the child who learns to read early is likely to have one or more older brothers and sisters or parents who read to him, and parents who are interested in the school. In a study by Plessas and Oakes (1964), only four parents of early readers worked outside the home. The good readers also reported owning more books than poor readers (Ramsey, 1962; Sheldon & Carillo, 1952).

A study (Van Zandt, 1963) of certain home-family-community factors related to children's achievement in reading in an elementary school showed that children in the highest quarter in achievement in fifth and sixth grades scored much higher than the lowest quarter in all sub-tests of the wisc, had more realistic educational and vocational aspirations, and were fortunate in having more favorable home and family conditions.

SOME SCHOOL VARIABLES

Many school conditions are obviously related to reading development and difficulties. Personality traits of teachers may be associated with children's reading failure. In relatively heterogeneous groups the following factors in teacher personality are reported as positive: intelligence, emotional stability, teaching competence, knowledge of the subject, a sympathetic and tactful manner, justice, discipline and order, social sense, ability to identify oneself with children, and interest in the teaching profession (Malmquist, 1960). Although these factors should be considered in diagnosis, the real relationship with reading disability may lie in one central characteristic or in the way in which the student perceives the teacher's behavior and attitude toward him.

Research on ecological factors, of which only a few examples have been given here, is useful to alert the teacher and clinician to conditions that might be facilitating or inhibiting a child's reading development. In a case-study approach, these and other central factors and patterns may be found to be significant for a given individual.

Neurological factors

Among the most deeply underlying causes of failure in reading are the neurological, chemical, and glandular. Failure to recognize neurological deficits and attempting to teach reading to children whose physical deficits make it impossible for them to learn is worse than useless; it often causes intense frustration with resulting passivity or aggression which interferes with later learning.

In this and related areas of diagnosis and remediation, Eames has published more than a hundred studies covering sensory, neurological, glandular, and general physical conditions. Eames (1960) summarized much of the research on both neurological and glandular bases of learning. Although more recent neurological research tends to de-emphasize the specific localization of brain functions and emphasizes the complexity of functioning of glands of internal secretion, Eames' review emphasizes the possible relationship of neural and glandular factors to reading performance.

Neurological dysfunction has frequently been related to laterality, i.e. disturbance in dominance of the two hemispheres of the brain.

The theory of cerebral dominance is based on inferences from observation of laterality in individuals. The relationship between laterality preference, which is observable behavior, and cerebral dominance, which is a postulate, requires further neurological clarification.

Handedness, left-eye dominance, mixed hand or eye dominance, crossed dominance, directional confusion, confusion in identifying right and left sides of the body have all been reported as related to reading disability. Two aspects that have been most frequently related to reading disability are: *1*] lateral preferences or inconsistency in hand and eye preference; *2*] spatial discrimination, i.e. failure to discriminate right and left or directional confusion.

As in other areas of investigation, results have been conflicting due to differences in degree of retardation studied, age of the child, bias in the selection of the sample, number of cases, and uncontrolled variables. However, certain relationships have been quite clearly established.

CEREBRAL DOMINANCE

The role of cerebral dominance in reading disability has been vigorously discussed since Orton's early article in 1928. Some investigators call attention to the relation between atypical laterality and backwardness in reading; a few deny that there is any relationship; others consider such a relationship, if it exists, to be insignificant. The relation of left-handedness and other lateral preferences to reading now seem to have been rejected by most investigators. Yet, it is possible that reading disability *may* be a basic biological defect. But, many ill-lateralized children do not have reading difficulties. More useful than correlations between tests of laterality and tests of reading achievement would be a study of the kind of disturbance in laterality associated with certain forms of reading disability.

Various tests of hand preference and directional confusion have been developed. Considerable information can be obtained from informal observation as in a play-therapy situation where the child plays with balls, throws darts, and engages in other activities.

Hand preference tests include directions and items such as those in the Harris Tests of Lateral Dominance (Harris, 1947-58). Each item is presented to the child as follows: "This is how I throw a ball (demonstrate). Now let me see you throw a ball." The items include directions to throw a ball, wind a watch, hammer a nail, brush teeth, comb hair, turn a doorknob, hold an eraser, cut with scissors, cut with a knife, and write. The hand used by the subject for each activity is recorded.

Eye preference is detected by looking through a kaleidoscope, rifle sighting, and looking through a hole in a paper at two pencils and paper clips. The eye used for each task is recorded.

The Van Riter Angle-Board Test was found to be a sensitive indicator of hand dominance and also to differentiate between good and poor readers.

Because of the continued concern about the relation of cerebral dominance to reading, several recent investigations are reviewed here.

Using the Harris Tests of Lateral Dominance, the Gates Reading Readiness Test, the Lorge-Thorndike Intelligence Test, and the Gates Primary Reading Tests of Word Recognition and Paragraph, I. H. Balow (1963) studied the relation between reading readiness, word recognition and paragraph reading, and the major dominance conditions: hand preference, eye preference, normal dominance, crossed hand and eye preference, mixed preference, knowledge of right and left (normal, hesitant, confused), mixed hand dominance (strong, moderate, mixed), knowledge of right and left, and interaction of factors. With 302 middle-class children beginning first grade, Balow found no significant relationship between dominance factors and reading readiness. Apparently first-grade children's hand or eye preference, dominance of hand and eye on the same side of the body, or mixed dominance was not related to reading readiness and achievement as measured. Balow concluded that "lateral dominance screening of children at the beginning of the first grade will not provide the teacher with information which will help her spot those children who are likely to have difficulty in learning to read" (1963, p. 328). Stevens, Cunningham, and Stigler (1967) also found that 89 first graders with crossed eye-hand preference appeared to function as well on the Metropolitan Reading Readiness Test as children with unilateral patterns of eye-hand preference. In summary, Stevens, Cunningham, and Stigler said that the results of their research

. . . do not substantiate the typical claims made concerning reading disability as a manifestation of mild neurological impairment. No results support the claims that mixed eye-hand preference patterns interfere with performance on measures of reading readiness. (1967, p. 486)

One investigation (Belmont & Birch, 1965) that avoided the limitations of many previous studies of this problem used subjects with I.Q.'s of 80 or above, drawn from the total population of Scottish school children born in 1953 in a single city. All children were tested thoroughly and individually. Laterality factors for normal and for retarded readers were then compared. Both groups were predominantly right-handed, and differences between the groups with respect to percentages who showed mixed dominance, eye dominance, and eye-hand dominance were not significant. Belmont and Birch concluded that:

The boys who were retarded in reading did not differ significantly in any type of mixed dominance from normal readers of the same age. Further, within each group no consistent relationship between lateral preferences and level of reading performance was found. (1965, p. 63)

Belmont and Birch's findings on lateralization differ from those of investigators who have studied retarded readers referred to clinics, but they are similar to those reported by other investigators who have drawn their samples from the general school population. In the clinic samples, difference in lateral dominance relations between normal and retarded readers have been found, but similar differences have not appeared in school or community populations. This may be due to the wide I.Q. range usually represented in clinics and the other social, neurological, and behavioral reasons for which children are referred to clinics.

Using a somewhat different battery of tests with boys in the fifth and sixth grades from a low socio-economic population who were retarded readers, Coleman and Deutsch (1964) likewise found no significant differences in hand, eye, or foot dominance or in any combination of these factors. Only 10 of the 121 subjects showed any indication of mixed hand dominance. Other investigations have also failed to find dominance conditions significantly associated with difficulties in reading (Silver & Hagin, 1960; Hillerich, 1966). Capobianco (1966) studied the effects of various patterns of laterality upon the performance of mentally-retarded adolescents (38 male, 20 female) on selected tests of reading. The subjects were educationally as well as mentally retarded and functioning two years below expectancy in reading. They showed a relatively high per cent (47 per cent) of non-established hand preference. However, the non-established laterality group, instead of experiencing more difficulty on the reading measures, surpassed the established laterality group on all reading tasks. Capobianco concluded that:

> . . . handedness and eyedness, at least for this mentally retarded population, bears no relation to reading achievement, and seemingly it relates negatively to performance which demands word recognition in traditional and mirror presentations. The determination of laterality preferences in this type of subject as part of a diagnostic work-up appears to possess dubious practical value. (1966, p. 785)

In view of the lack of definite relationship between laterality and reading, diagnostic information on this aspect seems of little importance, and the practice of trying to change children's laterality tendencies seems neither feasible nor desirable.

DIRECTIONAL ORIENTATION

Spatial and temporal orientation, however, seems to underlie all aspects of perception—visual, auditory, tactile, and kinesthetic. Such a relationship between reading and space-form and directional-sense deficiencies might be expected. The child who is handicapped in space-form perception would have difficulty in differentiating similarly formed letters such as *n* and *m*. The child with problems in directional orientation would be likely to confuse such letters as *f, t, p, b, g,* and *d,* and words like *pot* and *top*.

A number of investigations indicate a relationship between reading achievement and spatial orientation. Although lateral dominance bore no relation to reading, in Belmont and Birch's (1965) representative sample right-left awareness did. With respect to right-left, they found that:

> . . . the group of retarded readers included a greater number of children who were not able to identify right and left on own body parts with perfect accuracy, whereas only one of the normal readers failed to achieve a perfect score. . . This difference between groups was significant at the .01 level of confidence. (1965, p. 64)

The retarded readers who had difficulty in identifying right and left on their own bodies also had the lowest reading scores. The normal group performed in accordance with age specific expectation; the retarded group at the six-year-old level. This difference in the ability to locate right and left accurately apparently was not a function of verbal I.Q.. It seemed rather to be associated with differences in performance I.Q. In Coleman and Deutsch's (1964) study, the majority of fifth- and sixth-grade retarded readers on the Benton Right-Left Discrimination Test showed complete mastery of their own lateral schema but had more difficulty in recognizing that of other persons.

To study in another way the relationship between directional orientation and space-form perception and specific reading disability, Alexander and Money (1965) administered a reading test to seventeen patients with Turner's syndrome, "a cytogenetic disorder commonly manifesting a degree of space-form blindness and directional disorientation" (1965, p. 981). These patients proved not to be deficient in reading ability. Their mean reading age was close to their mean chronological age; the majority were at or above the mean. "Furthermore, there seemed to be no correlation between the severity of the neurocognitional deficits present and reading disability" (Alexander & Money, 1965, pp. 983-84). According to this study, space-form and directional deficiencies alone cannot account for specific reading disability.

Reversals and translocation of letters are errors common among all beginners in reading and writing. Usually they disappear after a few months. The potentiality for reversals, however, is never eliminated. In the school population which they studied, Belmont and Birch (1965) found reversals to be associated with poor reading on all four reading measures used. It would be interesting to know how thoroughly these children had been taught to read from left to right and to understand the difference in meaning that variation in position of letters makes.

Mirror writing. This is not a simple left to right reversal of letters and words as it is when you stand in front of a mirror and try to write your name on your own forehead; it is also near-and-far reversal. This confusion between visual and body images seems to underlie difficulties in directional orientation, just as difficulties in directional orientation may influence perception.

MATURATIONAL LAG

The parts of the brain (neopallium) which seem to control unilateral dominance, handedness, eyedness, visual and auditory symbol recognition, and spoken and written language show a wider range of maturation age than do other parts of the brain.

Children who present a picture of maturational lag may be identified by a slower developmental history, awkwardness, and uneven intellectual development. They may exhibit right-left confusion, immature personality, a family history of delay in the development of cortical dominance, and reading retardation (Bender, 1958; Cohn, 1964). Although these children tend to have an unstable perceptual background, they seem able to improve. They are not necessarily limited in potential; prognosis is favorable. When remedial techniques coincide with their needs, they overcome their reading disability.

NEUROLOGICAL DISORGANIZATION OR DYSFUNCTION

This condition differs from maturational lag in that its effects seem to be more resistant to remediation. Although no clear evidence of brain damage or neurological disease may be obtained in the diagnosis, the individual seems to have a basic difficulty in integrating written material and associating concepts with symbols. This condition has been frequently but erroneously labeled as "minimal brain damage." If no neurological evidence of brain damage has been detected, this label seems misleading.

Cohn (1964) has objected to equating minimal brain damage with minimal clinical signs because: *1*] certain clinical findings are "minimal" only by definition and context, *2*] a neurological relationship has not been demonstrated between minimal clinical signs and minimal brain pathology, *3*] the minimal clinical signs are dependent upon the test battery used and the philosophy of the experimenter. Therefore, since exact etiology of language disturbances remains unknown, Cohn believes that treatment must be non-specific and directed to utilizing the open or normal input channels.

Confusion and anxiety of parents and children have been caused by attributing, without sufficient evidence, reading difficulty to neurological impairment. This indiscriminate labeling has led to questionable practices in the treatment of reading difficulties. Reading specialists are not equipped to diagnose individuals with reading disabilities caused by cerebral pathology. Even outstanding neurologists are cautious in their diagnostic formulations.

Neurological dysfunction, not caused by brain damage, may account for reading and other learning disabilities. Its psychological effects may persist after the initial cause has ceased to exist. In adults, maturation, education, and other compensatory mechanisms may obscure the effects that early perceptual-motor problems may have had on reading disability.

Although no relationship may show up between neurological status and behavioral characteristics in general, specific subtests such as the WISC Mazes and Spelling and the Object Assembly and Auditory Blending did show increasing correlation with other variables on the basis of neurological classification (Boshes & Myklebust, 1964).

The electroencephalogram (EEG) is most often used to detect neurological disorganization. A much higher incidence of positive EEG findings has been reported in children with reading disabilities, as compared to the percentage in a matched group of normal children. However, the EEG is not always useful in determining the nature and extent of brain damage. When there is no actual cortical damage, the EEG findings may suggest only a delay in maturation. To diagnose children with neurological impairments is a most complex task. Many children have to be placed in a questionable category which should not be labeled as "minimal brain damage."

Visual perception tests, the Bender Visual-Motor Gestalt, the Marble Board, the Wepman Auditory Discrimination Test, and tests of laterality and body image are also used to detect neurological disorganization. A combination of developmental history and psychological and neurological tests is necessary in the diagnosis of neurological factors in reading disability. Diagnostic formulation based on all available data is necessary to plan appropriate educational experiences to be offered when the individual is ready for them. Early diagnosis is desirable,

for the brain in infancy and childhood is more plastic than in
later years and more able ot compensate for injury.

BRAIN DAMAGE

Neurologists no longer believe precisely pinpointed brain
areas are responsible for specific performance. Although in
. . . lesions of the angular gyrus the interpretation of
graphic signs is impaired or lost . . . areas adjacent to it do
stimulate processes involved in reading which is a learned
activity and needs a degree of instruction for functioning. . . . In reading we deal with the existence of highly
complex activities involving the whole brain. . . . For
reading comprehension, auditory language centers are extremely important. (de Hirsch, 1963, p. 278)

Even where definite brain damage has been determined by
neurological examination, the relation to reading and language
disabilities is not always evident. Many areas of the brain may
be implicated as possible sites of reading disability. New pathways may be substituted for the injured portions.

NEUROLOGICAL PATTERNS OR SYNDROMES

With reading disability cases, combinations of perceptual
and neurological symptoms occur more frequently than any
single cause. These cases have trouble with various types of
"gestalten;" their patterning of motor, visuo-motor, and perceptual configuration is often primitive (de Hirsch, 1963). These
patterns are detected only by a wide variety of tests and other
techniques. From a study based on 150 children with reading
disability and behavior disorders, Silver and Hagin (1960) obtained the following syndrome in 92 per cent or more of the
subjects: *1*] defects in right-left discrimination,   *2*] immature
and disorganized postural responses,   *3*] visual-motor imma-

turity with special angulation difficulty, and 4] visual figure-
background difficulty. A discrepancy between the writing hand
and the hand elevated on extension of the arms with eyes
closed seemed to have special diagnostic value. Bateman
(1966) reported that when a child shows the abnormality on
this test the chances are 96 to 100 that he has a reading problem. "If the test were found to be an effective predictor at age
five or six, it would probably replace the lengthy batteries which
are currently used with certainly no more than 90 per cent
efficiency and/or effectiveness" (Bateman, 1966, p. 104).

REMEDIATION

From the standpoint of neurological factors in reading disability, it is important to determine the defective areas in the
child's perceptual profile. Thus, it would be possible to give instruction and practice in the aspects of perceptual strength, to
use the avenues of learning or modalities through which he
learns most readily. At the same time, it would be important to
stimulate the defective areas. If a child confuses figure and
background, he should be protected, so far as possible, from
distractions in the classroom.

RELATION BETWEEN PERSONAL AND ENVIRONMENTAL FACTORS

The interaction between personal characteristics and needs
and the learning atmosphere and pressures of the environment
may be more closely related to reading performance than any
single aspect. An apparently similar environment will evoke different responses in different personalities.

McDonald (1961) reviewed the research on physical and
environmental factors that might be significantly related to reading disability. His excellent summary emphasized multicausal
factors: reading as a function of the whole personality and one
aspect of the growth of the individual; the importance of social

and personal adjustment in the treatment of reading disability in high school and college students; and the central importance of the self-concept. All of these pervasive factors should be considered in diagnosis and remediation. Some of the more recent research on these factors are summarized later.

Intelligence

THE RELATION OF INTELLIGENCE TO READING ACHIEVEMENT

To interpret test results, the teacher and clinician should know as much as possible about the nature of intelligence and the relation of intelligence tests to reading achievement. Of the three kinds of intelligence described by P. E. Vernon (1958a)—Intelligence A, which reflects the excellence of the functioning of the nervous system; Intelligence B, which is the result of the interaction between Intelligence A and the environment; and Intelligence C, which is a sample of some aspects of Intelligence B—only Intelligence A can be considered a possible cause of reading deficiency. Only Intelligence C is at present measured by intelligence tests, and there are as many Intelligence C's as there are tests.

Intelligence has long been considered a crucial factor in reading achievement; many research studies confirm this opinion. The results, however, vary with the instruments used to measure both intelligence and reading achievement. For example, both reading rate and reading comprehension, as measured by the Pressey Reading Rate and Comprehension Tests and the Iowa Tests of Basic Skills, are positively correlated with verbal and non-verbal intelligence sections of the Lorge-Thorndike Intelligence Tests, but more highly with the verbal than the non-verbal scores (Hage & Stroud, 1959).

Woodbury (1963) suggested a method to control some of the errors that make many differences between reading ages and mental ages misleading. He found that only divergencies larger than one year and five months between reading ages and mental ages may be truly significant. However, his method is too complex to be used by most teachers. Fransella and Gerver (1965) also presented elaborate equations to predict reading age on the Schonell Graded Word Reading Test. Winkley (1962) suggested as more useful than either of these methods a relatively simple formula such as "reading-expectancy grade = (years in school x I.Q.) + 1.0" or the discrepancy between the measure of potential and the measure of reading achievement of two stanine points, supplemented by "the subjective judgment of reliable and experienced teachers" (Winkley, 1962, p. 162).

It is logical to assume that the highest coefficients of correlation will be between the scores of group intelligence tests and silent reading tests. And, indeed, they are. Correlations ranging from .50 to .80 have been reported between silent reading tests and group intelligence tests. For example, the verbal intelligence test scores on the California Test of Mental Maturity correlated .824 with the Thorndike-McCall Reading Test, the quantitative scores, .557 (Strang, 1943). With ninth-grade pupils the correlations with reading ability were lower, but the ratio was about the same (Traxler, 1939). Oral reading tests used with elementary school children correlated lower, around .30 to .40 (Malmquist, 1960, p. 151). Bliesmer (1956) reported that poor readers exhibited significantly higher mean I.Q.'s on the Stanford-Binet than they showed on various group intelligence tests. Schiffman (1962), in a sample of sixty pupils referred to a remedial reading clinic, obtained a mean I.Q. of 79 from the California Test of Mental Maturity and a mean I.Q. of 95 from the WISC. Group intelligence test scores frequently reflect the handicapped reader's degree of retardation rather than his basic capacity to learn.

Two questions related to diagnosis were answered by Neville's study (1965). Does reading ability negatively influence I.Q. scores of pupils on a verbally-oriented group intelligence test? Obviously it does. In Neville's study, the poor fifth-grade readers scored higher on the individual tests requiring little or no reading; the average readers, about the same on both types of tests; and the good readers, as high or higher on the group test. The measures of intelligence that were used were the Lorge-Thorndike Intelligence Test; the WISC Verbal, Performance, and Full Scale scores; and the Peabody Picture Vocabulary Test. The Peabody Picture Vocabulary Test and the WISC gave similar results, especially for the average or poor readers. The mean Peabody I.Q. was not significantly different from the mean WISC Full Scale results.

What degree of reading deficiency is necessary to significantly lower the I.Q.? Neville (1965) found that a reading grade of 4.0 seems to be "a critical minimum for obtaining a reasonably valid I.Q. for children in intermediate grades" (1965, p. 260). From his findings, he concluded that a reading level below 4.0 tends to underestimate verbally-oriented group intelligence test results.

USE OF INTELLIGENCE TESTS IN FORMING READING GROUPS

It is common practice, when enrollment in remedial reading classes is limited, to select those students whose intelligence level is relatively higher than their reading level.

In some groups of pupils with special reading disabilities only a few have high intelligence scores. Schonell (1961) found this to be true in a group of 155 reading disability cases. In other groups a large proportion of the poor readers have either normal or superior intelligence. In Malmquist's (1960, p. 153) sample, 64.1 per cent were normal or above in intelligence. Bowers (1964) found that children in the primary grades who were making unsatisfactory progress in reading and arithmetic had intelligence test scores similar to norms for the WISC.

Recently doubt has been cast on the policy of excluding from remedial reading classes children with intelligence quotients below a certain level. Convincing evidence in favor of this point of view is accumulating. Frost (1963) studied two groups of children: children eight to ten years of age in seven remedial classes of twenty children each and children eleven to fifteen years old in groups of six in fifteen schools. These children were selected on the basis of a discrepancy of two years between their chronological age and reading age, as measured by the Schonell Graded Word Test and an I.Q. of 85 or higher on the Jenkins Non-verbal Intelligence Test and the Raven Progressive Matrixes. The use of these combined measures of intelligence as a selective procedure would have resulted in the exclusion of 36 and the inclusion of only 43 out of the 79 children who improved their reading age more than one and a half years. Apparently the children with the lower I.Q.'s benefited as much as the others from the remedial teaching. If such results were obtained with tests of good validity and reliability, what might be the detrimental results with tests of dubious reliability and validity used in many schools?

Additional doubt on the practice of excluding children with intelligence quotients below a certain level was reinforced by Chansky (1963b), who found an inverse ratio between I.Q.'s, as measured by the California Short Form Test of Mental Maturity, and the reading improvement of forty-one elementary school children who were in small remedial classes. The range in changes of reading scores was from —2 to +33 months. The correlation between I.Q. and reading improvement was .17, but when age was partialled out, it became —.35. The correlation between age and reading improvement was —.49. Using an adequate measure of intelligence such as is often used in schools, Chansky obtained

> . . . no empirical support was found for the belief that children with high I.Q.'s make the greatest progress in remedial reading. Rather age, or some correlate of it, perhaps history of failure or responsiveness to small-group instruction, was found to be related to improvement in reading. It appears to the writer that there is need to seek a criterion other than mental ability in making selections for class in Remedial Readers. (Chansky, 1963b, p. 439)

USE OF WISC SUB-TESTS FOR DIFFERENTIAL DIAGNOSIS

The use of WISC or WAIS sub-tests for differential diagnosis is promising. Many comparisons of retarded with normal readers on WISC and WAIS sub-tests have been reported (Coleman & Rasof, 1963; Hirst, 1960; Paterra, 1963; Sawyer, 1965). The majority of these studies have shown that retarded readers tend to be higher on the performance than on the verbal scale. On the California Test of Mental Maturity significant differences of 16 points or more between the verbal and the quantitative scores occurred in about one-fourth of the individuals tested (Mendenhall, 1959). More specifically, the retarded readers tended to be significantly lower on Information, Arithmetic, and Coding, and relatively high on Picture Arrangement, Block Design, and Object Assembly. Much of the knowledge and skill in the low areas are derived either from school or from reading. Coding scores might be expected to be low for retarded readers because coding requires visual discrimination and memory and closely resembles the decoding aspect of reading. A WISC profile typical of retarded readers with a low coding score is a diagnostic sign to consider in planning a remedial program.

Using deviation scores, i.e. the amount each subject deviated on each sub-test from his own average scaled score, M. S. Sheldon and Garton (1959) substantiated the findings of other investigators, showing that retarded readers were low on Arithmetic and Coding and relatively high on the Object Assembly sub-tests. The most disagreement seems to be with respect to the Vocabulary test scores which are low for some samples and relatively high for other samples of retarded readers.

There are variations in these results with different groups. For example, Ekwall (1966) found that in a group of retarded readers, bilinguals were significantly higher than the unilinguals in the sub-tests of Coding and Arithmetic and significantly lower on Information and Vocabulary. Different sub-tests also seem to play different roles when only boys are considered. Age, too, may make differences. Sawyer (1965) found that the ability of the sub-tests to discriminate between mildly and severely disabled readers decreased with age; discrimination seemed to be most effective at eight to ten years of age. Picture Completion was increasingly associated with the older, severely disabled readers.

The WAIS sub-test profile of unsuccessful readers is similar to that of psychopathic adolescents. Graham and Kamano (1958) found that the unsuccessful readers in a group of youthful criminals were inferior in verbal sub-tests and Digit Symbol. Their WAIS pattern was similar to that of the typical youthful psychopath. On the other hand, successful readers in the delinquent group did as well on verbal as on performance sub-tests. Their WISC pattern was different from that of psychopathic individuals. Some children can master the primary stage of word recognition and do well when concrete stimuli are presented to them, but they lack the mental abilities required in tests of Coding, Information, and Arithmetic, and in advanced reading.

OTHER TESTS OF INTELLIGENCE

The Wechsler Preschool and Primary Scale of Intelligence (WPPSI) (Wechsler, 1966), like the WISC, consists of a series of ability tests of various facets of a young child's intellectual competence. It contains six verbal tests and one alternate: Information, Vocabulary, Similarities, Comprehension, Arithmetic, and Sentences (alternate); and five performance tests: Animal House, Picture Completion, Mazes, Geometric Design, and Block Design. Norms are presented for eleven age levels, at three-month intervals from age 4 to 6½ years. The WPPSI is administered individually and requires from about forty-five minutes to one hour and fifteen minutes.

It is useful for the reading teacher and clinician to be familiar with several tests of intelligence that require no reading or language ability.

The Goodenough Draw-A-Man Test (DAMT) and the Harris Draw-A-Person Test continue to be useful. Both the original and the Goodenough and Harris (1963) revision of this test have moderate to good validity based on correlations with the WISC, Stanford-Binet, and California Mental Maturity Test. The correlations with group-test I.Q.'s were somewhat lower than those with individual I.Q. scores, and there was almost zero correlation between Draw-A-Man I.Q.'s and academic achievement test scores (Dunn, 1967b, p. 299). Dunn also found that the reliability of the Draw-A-Man Test was high— Pearsonian coefficients of .88 and .93 respectively for thirty-six boys and thirty-six girls in grades one through six. However, the scores produced by the Harris revised scoring procedure did not have greater reliability than those produced by the Goodenough method (Dunn, 1967a, p. 269). Scored according to the Goodenough instructions, the raw scores and the I.Q.'s on the DAMT showed correlations of .51 with the Gray-Votaw-Rogers Primary Achievement Test; .42 with reading comprehension; .30 with vocabulary; and .05 with chronological age. Girls scored higher than boys (Shipp & Loudon, 1964).

The Pictorial Test of Intelligence by Joseph L. French (1964), individually administered to children ages three to eight, requires only that children be capable of hearing and responding to verbal questions by pointing or looking at one of four pictures. Each of the six sub-tests measures several different facets of mental ability. This seems to be a promising test.

In general, short tests of intelligence are of doubtful validity. For the Ammons Quick Test, enthusiastically recommended by its publishers, Otto and McMenemy (1965) obtained correlations with the WISC too low for practical significance in the study of retarded readers. While not a substitute for the WISC, teachers have felt the Ammons Quick Test to be useful in obtaining quick estimates of the intelligence of poor readers. It can be administered in three to ten minutes. Its I.Q.'s tend to be higher than the WISC I.Q.'s. Since children perceive it as a game, it serves as a good rapport builder. By encouraging children's discussion of the answers, the teacher may gain a preview of pupils' verbal fluency and overanxiety about making errors.

Instead of using a new, poorly validated, quick intelligence test, the clinician might select a limited number of WISC sub-test

scores. By dropping the four least discriminating sub-tests—
Comprehension, Digit Span, Picture Completion, and Block Design—and retaining seven items, Sawyer (1965) found the ab-
breviated form useful in the early identification of children who
might have difficulty in learning to read.

Another possibility is to use just the vocabulary section of
the Stanford-Binet scale. When a full-scale individual verbal intelligence test is too time-consuming for use with large numbers
of children, "the best approximation to a verbal I.Q. is provided
by a vocabulary test. The WISC (1949) vocabulary sub-test correlates .89 with the verbal scale at 10½ years and .79 at 7½
years" (Ravenette, 1961, p. 97). The vocabulary section of the
Stanford-Binet has a similar correlation with the total Binet
score. Between the Crichton Vocabulary Scale and the Terman-
Merrill Scale, the correlation was .79 at nine years. The
Crichton Vocabulary Scale measures the ability to define words
when they are presented orally. The Schonell Graded Word
Reading Test measures the ability to define words when they
are presented visually. Ravenette estimated the degree of retardation in reading attainment by the magnitude of the discrepancy between these two tests.

CREATIVITY AND READING

Correlations between reading achievement and creativity
range from .13 to .37, the higher correlations being with measures of verbal creativity. From the studies thus far available, it
would seem that a test of creativity need not be included in the
diagnosis of reading achievement. However, certain creativity
variables that may be important to reading achievement are not
measured by intelligence tests (Robinson, Weintraub, & Smith,
1966).

In an intensive study, using introspection and retrospection
of highly creative and highly intelligent secondary-school students, Stemmler (1966) found differences in their reading

styles. The highly creative individual read with much more imagination and sensitivity to the author's style and characterization and to the mood and tone of the passage. He "generated many speculations while reading," created new situations and became a part of the author's experiences. He seemed to have read more "from within" than "from without." In contrast, the highly intelligent individual was more realistic; he systematically compared and contrasted essential components of a passage, secured the meanings of the passages with speed and efficiency.

In appraising the individual's capacity for more subtle and insightful interpretation of literature, the teacher or diagnostician should explore those aspects of creativity not included in either intelligence or reading tests.

These studies suggest the following diagnostic inferences:

1] Retarded readers, as a group, because of difficulty in handling abstractions, tend to approach learning situations in a concrete manner.

2] They do less well in areas resembling school learning (Arithmetic, Vocabulary, Coding). They show limited ability to concentrate.

3] They are not inherently less endowed in some capacities but fail to develop these capacities because of their reading disability.

4] Their reading may be improved more through verbal reasoning than from vocabulary study that depends solely upon memorization.

5] The underachiever may be significantly higher than the average on incidental learning (Comprehension and Picture Completion) and on perceptual organization (Block Design).

6] The ability of the WISC sub-tests to differentiate degrees of reading disability decreases with age.

Sub-test scores and patterns of sub-test scores on the WISC and the WAIS may be useful indicators of potential reading ability. They call attention to possible strengths and weaknesses in mental abilities that may underlie reading achievement in individual cases and in groups of retarded readers. Ekwall (1966) developed a simple method of making individual profiles which would indicate strengths and weaknesses in these underlying mental abilities as a basis for remedial measures. Since intellectual factors interact with other factors, such as level of anxiety, profiles that include more than intelligence are needed. Children with reading problems may also have poor auditory memory and sound-blending ability and problems in right-left discrimination of their own bodies and those of other people. They may also be deficient in the integration of visual and auditory stimuli (Birch & Belmont, 1964). Some have had unfavorable educational experiences.

Mental test performance seems to predict mature reading best. As soon as the child goes beyond the stage of decoding printed symbols, reading becomes a reasoning process and intelligence an important factor in his success. Bond and Tinker (1957) reported a correlation between intelligence and reading tests of .35 at the end of the first grade and .65 at the end of the sixth grade. Others have reported similar increases in correlations from the primary grades, in which sensory-motor and perceptual abilities predominate, to the upper grades which demand abstract verbal abilities.

Thus, the role of intelligence varies with the child's stage of reading development. It may be of least importance in beginning reading when the task is predominantly one of visual and auditory perception. It soon becomes more important as the integration of auditory and visual perception becomes necessary in word recognition; intelligence is involved still more in the combining of perceptions into concepts. It is of major importance in sentence and paragraph reading which requires the weighing and relating of ideas.

Personality and emotional factors in reading disability

There is a wide divergence of views about the role of personality factors in reading disability. At one extreme, a small percentage of reading disorders is attributed to emotional disturbances; at the other extreme, very few reading problems are attributed to personal maladjustment. Ackerman (1936, p. 310) observed that "children with seemingly arrested learning ability exhibit personality deviations with extraordinary frequency and that the whole child, not the retardation, must be treated." This view emphasizes the building of ego strength as a means of increasing reading ability. Success in any aspect of life tends to increase general self-confidence and effort in attacking reading tasks.

Reading disability is often considered a symptom of existing conflicts in the individual. These may cause failure in learning to read. On the other hand, failure to learn to read may give rise to emotional disturbances. One aggravates the other: emotional disturbance leading to more difficulty in reading and that, in turn, intensifying the emotional disturbance. Personality maladjustment may be the cause, the result, or a concomitant of reading disability.

PERSONALITY PATTERNS OF POOR READERS

The teacher's and clinician's understanding of the relationship between reading achievement and personality traits and emotional disturbance shapes to a great extent diagnostic and remedial procedures.

Since 1953 more than one hundred experimental studies of the relationship between personality and reading ability have been reported. Differences in specific personality traits between good and poor readers reported by some studies are often contradicted by others. The relationships found seem to vary with the age of the subject: more positive traits in the earlier years, more negative at the high school and college levels. Lack of self-confidence and self-reliance, instability, and timidity seemed to be characteristic of children in the primary grades, and withdrawal tendencies of some elementary children, but not of children in the intermediate grades. Using the California Test of Personality, Norman and Daley (1959) found no difference in patterns of adjustment between inferior and superior readers among sixth-grade boys. However, the retarded readers expressed stronger feelings of rejecting and being rejected by others but, at the same time, they longed for acceptance. During junior high school the poor readers seemed to be less well adjusted to school routines and not so popular with their peers as good readers. In senior high school and college, differences between good and poor readers in personality characteristics were not so clearly indicated. For example, a study of 161 males and 87 female poor readers (Raygor & Wark, 1964) showed that on the Minnesota Multiphasic Personality Inventory (MMPI) the poor readers showed symptoms characteristic of the neurotic personality. The general college population, however, also had home conflicts with mother, insomnia, and poor rapport with counselors. The male poor readers had less verbal ability and were, in general, less comfortable in social situations, more shy and withdrawn, and somewhat more immature. They had a greater need for social acceptance than the average college population. The female poor readers, on the other hand, appeared to be better adjusted than the average. They were more emotionally healthy; less depressed, withdrawn, and introverted; generally less tense and uncomfortable. There was only one whose score on the MMPI approximated that of a psychiatric patient. Another investigator (Neal, 1964), using the MMPI with college sophomores, also found a relationship between reading disability and certain neurotic aspects of personality even in a highly able population.

These findings led Holmes (1961, p. 113) to hypothesize that "there may be, in fact, an actual 'gradient shift' in the relationship between personality factors and reading disabilities as children advance through the grades." He also pointed out on

the basis of further research that "discrepancies between parental attitudes about their children and children's self-attitudes
may be more important for school learning than the child's attitudes about himself" (1961, p. 117). Another insight gained
from the Holmes' studies was that school success may be related
to certain factors that are commonly described as "maladjustment," such as introversion and a tendency to brood a great
deal. Underlying success in a complex ability like reading may
result from "a deep-seated value system, the presence of which
facilitates the functional organization of those subskills." This
basic motivation Holmes (1961, p. 120) describes as
"mobilizers"—the many attitudes that the individual holds toward the purpose of life, duty, adversities, and the self.

A deeper understanding of personality configurations of retarded readers has been obtained from clinical studies and
projective techniques by Blanchard (1928), Challman (1939),
Ephron (1953), Staiger (1961), Vorhaus (1952), and Mc-
Donald, Zolik, and Byrne (1959). For example, Vorhaus (1952)
administered the Rorschach tests to 309 retarded readers, both
boys and girls six to fifteen years old. From analysis of the test
data, four unique personality patterns, or patterns of response
became evident:

1] The individual's principal way of adapting to life is to
   repress his inner drives. This inhibits growth; he lacks
   spontaneity.

2] The individual lacks emotional responsiveness to the
   external world. The pleasure drives he feels are not
   acted out.

3] The creative talents which the individual possesses are
   not acted out.

4] The individual is responsive to stimulation but feels that
   it is necessary to repress these strong feelings. He is
   afraid of his feelings of anger and may turn them inward
   against himself. (Vorhaus, 1952)

Similar characteristics were reported in a more recent study of thirty-five fourth-grade children (Silverman, Fife, & Mosher, 1959). Projective techniques are more likely to reveal deep-seated personality traits; the paper-and-pencil personality tests are subject to errors due to lack of understanding of oneself and the wording of the items, a common desire to make a good impression, and other factors.

There is a little support, mostly clinical, of the psychoanalytical theory of the association of reading disability with fear and avoidance of looking; hostility, primarily toward the parent of the same sex; and failure to identify with parents of the same sex. However, an alternative interpretation in terms of parental conditioning of exploratory and sexual responses is also feasible (Walters, Van Loan, & Crofts, 1961).

OTHER EFFECTS OF PROLONGED READING DISABILITY

It is generally assumed that children who experience initial difficulty in learning to read have feelings of inadequacy in the classroom where success becomes increasingly difficult to attain without skill in reading. Cases of 16 primary and 16 preadolescent reading problems (Robeck, 1964) showed some common characteristics, chief among which was extreme tension and emotional involvement in connection with reading. Both age groups lacked word-attack skills; both had limited verbal capacity on the WISC but showed strength in the WISC sub-tests of Comprehension, Similarities, Picture Completion, Picture Assembly, and Block Design. On the California Test of Personality, however, none of the primary children and only one of the older group made abnormal scores. More than half of both age groups expressed dissatisfaction with teachers, school, and fellow students. Robeck also found that certain other correlates of reading difficulty—hyperactivity, distractibility, and confused lateral dominance—tended to disappear by puberty, but poor recall of auditory symbols, lack of auditory discrimination, poor visual recall, the effect of early school entrance, and family pressure to

succeed in school tended to persist throughout elementary school
years and adolescence. Frequent interruptions in school, lack of
physical vitality, and low self-esteem tended to be associated
with reading disability more frequently during adolescence than
earlier.

RELATION OF ANXIETY TO READING DISABILITY

Considerable attention has been given to the role of anxiety in reading-disability cases. It is a common symptom and
probably has a reciprocal relationship with reading disability:
the more anxiety, the more interference with reading; the
greater the difficulty with reading, the more anxiety.

The Children's Manifest Anxiety Scale (CMAS) is the instrument most frequently used to measure children's anxiety.
Reger (1964) found this test to be fairly reliable with retarded
children. They scored significantly higher than non-retarded
subjects, and institutionalized retarded children scored higher
than similar children attending public schools. (A high score indicates a high degree of anxiety.) Different methods of administering the CMAS may yield different results. Since the results also
vary with cultural differences, school atmosphere, and with
rural, suburban, and city environments, one must be cautious in
comparing results in one situation with those in another.

The relation of anxiety to achievement has been studied
extensively. This factor may influence the diagnostic process as
well as achievement in reading and other school subjects. Apparently, complicated skills such as reading suffer more interference from anxiety than do simpler memory tasks such as spelling.

Pacheco (1964) found a high level of anxiety among
sixth-grade children related to low achievement in reading comprehension and vocabulary, although anxiety tended to affect
their reading comprehension more than their vocabulary. In a
study of mentally retarded children, Reger (1964) did not find
as clear-cut evidence of the relationship of anxiety to achievement.

With nine-year-old children, Cowen, Zax, and Klein (1965) obtained correlations between scores on the Child Manifest Anxiety Test of —.26 with the SRA reading comprehension, and —.23 with reading vocabulary, both of which were at the .01 level of significance. A similar negative correlation was obtained with intelligence as measured by the California Mental Ability Scale.

Anxiety seems to be pervasive. Among nine-year-old children, anxiety was related to teachers' rating of maladjustment, to discrepancies between their self-concept and self-ideal, and to a tendency to assume and accept negative roles in a sociometric situation and to complain about physical disabilities (Cowen, Zax, & Klein, 1965).

Anxiety may be aroused or intensified by unclear questions, explanations, and assignments. If the reading task is unfamiliar or ambiguous in its structure, the detrimental effects of anxiety become more evident.

High anxiety affected the speed and comprehension of fourth-grade boys, even though they were at or above their fourth-grade level in reading ability (Gifford & Marston, 1966). They were lacking in flexibility and did not adapt their reading speed appropriately to the purpose for reading. The highly anxious boys may have needed more time for the integrating and abstraction process required in getting the author's pattern of thought. A pre-testing practice experience was helpful in giving them a sense of structure which enabled them to read at a more normal speed.

Anxiety is more likely to affect achievement than intelligence. With both nine-year-old children and sixth-grade pupils, Frost (1965) obtained a negative correlation between anxiety and achievement and a positive correlation between anxiety and intelligence. The more intelligent have less need to feel anxious about their school achievement if they have a history of success.

There are a number of indications of undue tension that teachers can observe in pupils while they are reading. Robeck (1962a), on the basis of her study of twenty reading clinic cases

7.1 to 14.8 years old with I.Q.'s of 93 to 130, mentioned the following: tautness of posture, strained voice, paleness or flushed face, perspiration on forehead, increased stammer, random movements, deterioration of rapport, and sighing. During oral reading, the tense readers showed fewer errors than the control group; their fluency errors were about half the total errors for both groups. They tended to substitute words with like beginnings and similar configurations that made sense in the context, though they showed little evidence of looking for context clues. They would substitute another word rather than have it supplied. The tense readers tended to stop when they had made an error. Frequent errors resulted in a marked increase in tension symptoms. The tense readers and the ones who lacked word-recognition skills had similar profiles on the WISC sub-tests except in Picture Assembly where the non-tense were strong and the tense, weak.

High anxiety can disorganize behavior. Children conditioned early to high levels of anxiety have difficulty in attending to new learning stimuli. Their anxiety mounts as they are unable to fix their attention on the learning task. As anxiety increases, their responses become less accurate and this creates still more anxiety. They need to associate the reading situation which is causing anxiety with a friendly, relaxed atmosphere, a warm relationship, and other positive stimuli which are "incompatible with anxiety and thus inhibit the anxiety response" (Reger, 1964, p. 654).

Manifest anxiety is only part of a personality pattern that may decrease a person's ability to understand and deal effectively with new situations. Weitzner, Stallone, and Smith (1967) found that college students with high anxiety had a low self-opinion; felt that others had an unfavorable and incorrect opinion of them; were dependent upon encouragement, sympathy, and affection; felt inferior toward others in most respects, and were more aware of the conditions operating in a particular situation. These characteristics might tend to reduce effort and result in perfunctory performance in reading tasks.

RELATION OF THE SELF-CONCEPT TO READING ACHIEVEMENT

The self-concept is what the person thinks himself to be. Although the self-concept develops to some extent during school years, it is resistant to change. As a central core or radix of personality, which has a persistent, pervasive influence on all aspects of the individual's life, it would obviously be related to reading achievement, Schwyhart (1967) reviewed the substantial evidence that such a relationship exists. In general, children with high or mature self-concepts tend to achieve higher in proportion to their potential, as measured on an intelligence test, than do children with low self-concepts. This tendency was evident as early as kindergarten, and continued through elementary school, and among college students. It seems as though the self-concept shapes an individual's approach to reading.

The relationship between perception of self and utilization of intellectual ability is circular—one reinforces the other. The self-rejecting individual is poorly motivated. He gives up too easily and cannot keep his mind on his work. It often seems as though children who come to reading clinics cannot read because they believe they cannot read. When they are helped to succeed in simple reading experiences, they begin to see themselves as readers, and their attitude toward themselves improves.

The improvement of the self-concept might be expected to lead to improvement in reading, and improvement in reading to a more positive self-concept. Both reading improvement and a more positive self-concept might be facets of a central core of personality or ego strength. Which aspect should be emphasized would depend upon a diagnosis of the situation. It would depend on the origins of the reading difficulty and the self-concept, the special skill of the teacher in reading instruction or mental health, and the composition of and relationships within the class group.

Although the diagnostic significance of the self-concept for reading improvement is so crucial, a measure of the self-concept is difficult to obtain. It cannot be studied directly but only through the responses an individual makes about himself, or unconsciously reveals in a projective-type technique, or through inferences based on observation of his behavior. Intimate contacts with students over a year's time would offer opportunities for the alert teacher and the case worker to appraise an individual's self-concept with reference to his reading progress.

A number of ways of assessing the self-concept have been developed. Schwyhart (1967) found that each of five measures of the self-concept gave a somewhat different slant on the self-concept as a whole. A sentence-completion technique developed specifically for reading diagnosis (Strang, McCullough, & Traxler, 1967) gave clues as to the students' attitudes toward their family, themselves, school, and reading. The self descriptions—'the kind of person I think I am; the kind of person other people think I am; and the kind of person I want to be"—which gave the individual freedom to present himself in his own way, uninfluenced by any stimulus words, tended to evoke the individual's idiosyncratic or unique ideas and feelings. The Q-sort of Adjectives (Lipsitt, 1958; Shaw, Edson, & Bell, 1960) offered opportunity for specific self-appraisal of characteristics, which the subjects selected as "like me," "not like me," and "not sure."

The self-portrait technique which merely asked the student to "draw a picture of yourself" was interpreted by a clinical psychologist, Dr. Helen Williams, who had had much experience in the analysis of figure drawings. Dr. Williams' interpretations sometimes reinforced and sometimes modified impressions obtained by other techniques. They were probably on the subjects' unconscious level. To get at the subjects' conscious self, the examiner might ask them to describe their drawings and/or answer the question, "Who are you?" The self-portrait data frequently dealt with deeper emotions and problems of establishing identity.

The interview data varied with a number of factors, such as the relationship of the interviewer to the interviewee; his skill in eliciting accurate, frank responses and in encouraging introspection; the setting; and both parties' understanding as to the purpose and use of the data being collected. Occasionally partially presented insights could be followed as Piaget did in his studies. The interview was especially useful in getting a history of school experiences as these students perceived them.

Thus, each technique may make a unique contribution to a global understanding of the individual's self-concept. A combination of techniques is essential in obtaining well-rounded descriptions.

Two unique methods of obtaining information about the way a child thinks about himself were developed by Bower (1960). The first was an introspective report which Bower called TAY: Thinking About Yourself. The other was a two-part sociometric measure calling for: *1*] a free response on which a sociometric estimate could be made; and   *2*] a list of thirty possible roles, half positive and half negative, from which the child selects four that he would like to play.

SEVERE EMOTIONAL DIFFICULTIES

Emotional disturbances do not necessarily interfere with learning. Some students achieve adequately in spite of severe emotional disturbances. On the other hand, reading problems have been identified in a large per cent of the children and adolescents who have been institutionalized for emotional disturbance or delinquency. Bender (1958) pointed out parallels between children with severe reading disability and schizophrenia. The schizophrenic child is uncertain because of his poorly defined ego boundaries; the dyslexic child, because of his inability to deal with symbols.

Shimota (1964) studied 74 emotionally disturbed children and adolescents admitted to Western State Hospital. Their ages ranged from 13.0 to 15.11, and their I.Q.'s were at least 80 on the Wechsler Full Scale. Of these children, 43.2 per cent had developed adequate reading skills; 31.1 per cent showed reading performance 25 per cent or more below the expected grade placement. The boys were more often retarded than the girls. The performance I.Q.'s of the disabled readers were markedly higher than their verbal I.Q.'s. Among the adequate readers,

forty per cent of the girls (but none of the boys) had performance I.Q.'s fifteen or more points above their verbal scores.
Using the Rabinovitch classification *1*] organic damage, *2*]
primary reading retardation associated with basic capacity necessary to associate concepts with symbols and to integrate written material, and *3*] secondary reading retardation associated
with emotional disturbance or an inadequate learning situation
—Shimota studied the incidence of various symptoms usually
associated with neurological factors in each of the three groups.
Only three of the variables, thought to be related to primary
reading retardation, differentiated the adequate from the disabled readers. The symptoms alone or in combination failed to
differentiate between the two groups. However, more of the adequate readers had visual problems and a higher incidence of
atypical birth history. The groups did not differ on eye-hand coordination, speech problems, postnatal head injury, or dominance. In this study, almost all the factors studied occurred as
frequently in the able as in the disabled readers. Shimota (1964,
p. 108) suggested that "the interaction of some teachers and
some methods with some pupils produces reading disability."

Reading patterns and success or failure during primary
years may have emotional origins during pre-school years. Carrithers (1965) obtained a classification of emotional status of
61 pre-school children with I.Q.'s of 115 to 120 from a psychologist, a social worker, and a teacher who worked with the children daily. There was much disagreement among these three
persons from the three different points of view, but the compos-
ite picture may have given the more complete estimate of emotional problems. Carrithers concluded that:

> The children with emotional difficulties, determined at the
> pre-school level, have greater difficulty in learning to read
> than those without such problems, and that the reading dif-
> ficulty stays with them throughout the primary grades.
> (1965, p. 6)

However, these children showed different growth patterns. The
problem group, which was slowest at the start and made no
measurable gain during the first semester, made the greatest

spurt during the second and third semesters and gradual growth from then on; their less positive initial attitudes changed by the third grade. Those without emotional difficulties made gains from the beginning, took a spurt after they got started, and continued to increase in reading ability. The group in between the two extremes made quite steady progress throughout the two years.

Emotional factors give clues as to the characteristics of poor readers who are most likely to profit by remedial work. To study the relationship between twenty-two variables and reading achievement, Krippner (1966b) used the California Reading Test, the Mental Health Analysis (MHA), and the Holtzman Inkblot Technique (HIT). The correlations between the inkblot and the MHA scores were high enough to suggest that children in grades two-six with "disordered thought processes, bizarre perceptions, and emotionally disturbing fantasies" (Krippner, 1966b, p. 522) would be likely to be distracted by their own thoughts instead of giving their attention to the reading task. Their perceptions are often distorted by misinterpretation of stimuli and they may tend to concentrate on insignificant details.

Using the Thematic Apperception Test (TAT) with 48 good and 48 poor readers, Woolf (1962) found that poor readers expressed physical aggression more often and more intensely than the situation would justify. They had a greater desire and need for encouragement and affiliation than the poor readers and were more hesitant to make a decision or trust their own judgment. They were also consistently higher in the number of needs they expressed. The poor readers also seemed less well adjusted in a dominant role and felt a definite lack of affection from families and peers. They tended to be more inhibited and gloomy, more stereotyped. Such emotional factors seem to interact with reading disability, one intensifying the other.

IMPLICATIONS FOR GUIDANCE

Success in reading may be markedly affected by personality factors: attitudes, feelings, prejudices, and general adjustment of the reader. Fears and worries tend to be more prevalent among retarded readers than among advanced readers. According to one view, reading retardation is a symptom of emotional difficulties and is related to the severity of the emotional disturbance. If diagnosis and remedial work are to be successful, they must take these affective factors into consideration. However, therapy, while making the individual more accessible to learning, is ineffective in improving reading unless it is accompanied by competent instructon and appropriate practice in the reading skills needed by the individual.

There is evidence that group and individual therapy is helpful in dealing with certain reading problems (McDonald, Zolik, & Byrne, 1959). Using nine tests of intelligence, reading achievement, and personality to collect the data, McDonald and his associates reported that college students who had therapy sessions of one and one-half hours per week in addition to their regular remedial reading periods improved in speed and comprehension of reading, became more flexible in speed and method of approach, and showed less discrepancy among their self-concepts, the concepts of others, and their ideal self. The changes in self-concept and concept of others were very marked, over and above the control group which did not have the group therapy sessions. They also made improvement in grade-point averages and maintained the improvement a year later. They had become more self-motivated toward achievement in college. In combination with the methods of reading instruction used in this experiment, group psychotherapy contributed significantly to a college reading improvement program.

Any diagnosis that does not explore personality factors that may influence reading achievement is inadequate.

3. *Severe reading disabilities (dyslexia)*

Neurologists and physiologists often attribute cases of severe reading disabilities to brain damage or to a more general brain dysfunction. This approach rests on an insecure basis (Cohn, 1964). It is discouraging because educators can do nothing specifically and directly about actual brain injury. The result is that remedial measures are often used on a trial-and-error basis in the treatment of children with these severe reading difficulties.

A thorough, detailed review of the literature from medical and psychiatric as well as from psychological and educational sources was published in 1959 by Kawi and Pasamanick. In addition, a study of 372 white male children with reading disorders was undertaken to test the hypothesis "that some of the reading disorders in childhood may be consequent to minimal cerebral injury following abnormalities of the prenatal and paranatal periods" (Kawi & Pasamanick, 1959, p. 3). The results of this study indicated "that there exists a relationship between certain abnormal conditions associated with childbearing and the subsequent development of reading disorders in the offspring" (Kawi & Pasamanick, 1959, p. 61).

Cerebral injury may be caused by complications of pregnancy, delivery, and the neo-natal period. It may result from *1*] maternal rubella and other toxemias of pregnancy; *2*] Rh isoimmunization, certain drugs, maternal nutrition, and other factors that could influence intrauterine life; *3*] difficult or prolonged labor, oxygen deprivation, and premature birth.

Reversals, confusion of letters, disfigurements of letters, and similar errors in reading occur in normal children during their first school years; but, in pathological cases, these errors in writing are not overcome. These same errors also occur in patients with Gerstmann's syndrome and "constitute one of the symptoms of the patient's organic cerebral lesion" (Hermann,

1956, p. 181). Hermann concluded that the characteristic feature of both word-blindness and Gerstmann's syndrome is impairment of a sense of direction in space—right-left uncertainty.

Classification and terminology

Rabinovitch's (1959) classification is useful in differentiating cases of severe reading disability:

1] Organic cases. In these cases, the capacity to learn to read is impaired by clear-cut neurological deficits diagnosed as brain damage. This damage may be caused by prenatal toxicity, birth trauma, anorexia (oxygen deprivation), or head injury.

2] Primary cases. In these, the capacity to read is believed to be impaired, but specific evidence of brain damage is not obtained. An assumption is that these cases may be caused by a disturbed pattern of neurological organization or functioning or maturational lag.

3] Secondary cases. In these, the physiological capacity is intact, but it is not utilized sufficiently for the child to read up to his mental potential. This kind of disability may be due to unfavorable or limited educational experiences, visual or auditory impairment, or emotional problems such as negativism, anxiety, depression, or emotional problems of other kinds.

Various words have been used to describe cases of severe reading disability. Definitions of these terms are listed below.

Alexia: inability to identify verbal symbols. The person suffering from alexia can see the letters; his intellect is unimpaired, but he has lost the ability to read, understand, and interpret printed or written symbols. It is sometimes described as "visual aphasia."

Dyslexia: a severe reading retardation which exists despite adequate instruction and is not due to poor motivation, mental retardation, emotional disturbance, or sensory defects.

Word blindness: a form of congenital visual aphasia; this term is used in Denmark and Sweden.

Strephosymbolia: twisted or misplaced symbols.

Brain damage: any injury to the brain structure. Alternate terms: brain injury, organic brain damage.

Cerebral dysfunction or impairment: neurological disturbance, not definitely identified with actual brain injury.

Prevalence

As with other causes of retardation in reading, there is variation in the incidence of neurological factors reported. Estimates vary from 1 per cent in one school population, 4 to 10 per cent in other populations, 20 per cent in a clinic population, to 75 per cent in a study by Penn (1966). One out of ten is the figure most frequently quoted as the proportion of severely retarded readers who may be neurologically impaired. This variation in estimates of incidence depends not only on the sample but on the depth of the diagnosis and the point of view of the investigator.

Correlates or causes

Instead of seeking neurological causes of those reading problems that baffle teachers, parents, and clinicians, a more fruitful approach seems to be one in which "an effort is made to discover psychological correlates of reading disability. Hope-fully, this should lead to more specific remedial procedures" (Kass, 1966, p. 533).

A number of factors have been shown to be related to reading difficulty, but causal relationship is difficult to prove. Although there are many differences in terminology and etiol-ogy, there is agreement on certain typical characteristics asso-ciated with, but not exclusive to, severe reading disability: a general visuo-perceptual deficit; slow rate of cerebral develop-ment; general intellectual backwardness; physical, including neurological, impairments; general retardation and difficulties in speech and specific language; and personality factors, uncon-trollable emotions, and decreased emotional tolerance. The lit-erature is quite inconsistent with respect to the role of form per-ception and directional sense in severe reading disabilities. The effect of deficiencies in these areas varies with the age and intel-ligence of the child. Inferior form perception, visuo-motor skill, and directional sense may play a significant role in reading re-tardation in the early school years. They should always be in-cluded in the appraisal of a severe reading problem. "But it does not seem that they can be made to account for more than a small proportion of the cases presented by older children" (Benton, 1962, p. 101).

Reading difficulties seldom occur singly. Organic defects may contribute to reading disabilities; heredity also plays a part. Multiple regression analyses have shown a relationship between certain combinations of characteristics and neurological findings such as the WISC mazes and spelling; the WISC Object Assembly and auditory blending; social maturity, auditory blending, and spelling. No single relationship between neurological status and behavior characteristics has been found. It is often difficult to distinguish primary causes from the consequences of the reading disability. Even when there is actual brain injury, intelligence and reading achievement are not always affected; there have been cases who have retained a high I.Q. after portions of the cortex have been removed.

Even less clear-cut are biological disturbances of neurological organization associated with inability to deal with integration of symbols—a generalized brain dysfunction rather than a specific lesion. Cohn (1964) considered the case for "minimal brain damage" as not totally convincing.

Maturational lag may result in slower development of language skills, especially reading, and lead to severe reading problems. This lag is much more frequent among boys than among girls.

Although the hypothesis that there is some nervous system disorder associated with severe reading difficulties has been supported by many authorities, it now seems clear that in these cases psychological factors may be interfering more than physiological with performance and learning. However, although there is disagreement about specific causes of dyslexia, the existence of a syndrome or pattern of behavioral symptoms has been described.

Behavioral manifestations

If severe reading disability is considered a symptom of diverse conditions, then the need for a meaningful system of differential diagnosis seems obvious (Benton & Bird, 1963). However, it is exceedingly difficult to make a differential diagnosis of specific dyslexia. This problem arises in the less severe cases: "No one has as yet uncovered any tell-tale sign or group of signs that are exclusive to the syndrome of specific dyslexia and are not found in other conditions of reading retardation" (Money, 1962, p. 16). It is necessary to depend upon:

> . . . the clinical appraisal of the whole configuration of symptoms and test findngs. . . . Whatever the etiology of reading retardation, the known principles and stages of therapy are the same. (Money, 1962, p. 17)

The ranges of normality and abnormality are wide.

Severe reading disability seems to be associated with a wide variety of other communicative disorders including impairment in hearing, deviations in speech, voice problems, and language disorders. It is associated with maturation of the cognitive process and with emotional disturbance often as an effect rather than as a cause.

Any combination of the following characteristics may be found in cases of severe reading disability (Myklebust & Johnson, 1962; Money, 1962; Money, 1966; Krippner & Herald, 1964; Silver & Hagin, 1960, 1966):

Perceptual skills

    Poor visual perception as shown in the WISC coding and mazes

    Perception of only initial letters of a word

    Difficulty with certain similar letters such as *b-d, v-u*

    Reversal of letters, words, and phrases

        "The dyslexic individual is not unique in making reversals and translocations, but he is unique in making so many of them for so long a time" (Money, 1962, p. 17).

    Mirror writing

    Perceptual errors in reading and spelling

    Difficulty in distinguishing figure from ground; these cases are extremely attentive to background stimuli; they may perceive everything as equally significant and grasp only exceptionally dominant aspects. They have difficulty in focusing on words in context[1]

    Frequent omission of vowels when writing

Psychomotor disturbance

    Confused directionality and left-right orientation*

    Distorted body image*

    Immature or disorganized postural responses*

    Visual-motor immaturity

    Difficulty in motor coordination

    Inability to write until after they have learned to read

    Poor drawing and copying ability

Auditory perception and speech

    Deficiencies in auditory discrimination

---

*Found in 92 per cent or more of the cases (Silver & Hagin, 1960).

Difficulty with certain similar sounds such as *p-b, g-v*
Slow speech development. Reading difficulty
"would be closely related to a speech disability if a
child is poor in auditory development and is approaching
reading in a phonetic method" (Wepman, 1962, p. 183).
Sound blending, sound matching problems

Mental abilities

Deficiencies in memory and association—very important in
relation to orientation and such abstractions as time,
size, number, direction.
WISC verbal I.Q. averaging more than twenty points lower
than performance

Emotional factors
Marked anxiety and frustration

Academic retardation

Less favorable response to remedial instruction; less progress
from day to day

Usually older than the average child in their grade
Some children will fit into the above categories; others will not.
However, the differences seem to be quantitative and in the degree, rather than in the kind of error. There seems to be a continuous gradation from the poorest to the best reader (Malmquist, 1960).

However, there seems to be no clearly established greater
incidence of left-hand preference, ambilaterality, left-or-right-
eyedness, or mixed dominance in the disabled reader. A discrepancy in response between the writing hand and the hand elevated on extension of the arms, with eyes closed, appears to be
closely associated with reading problems (Silver & Hagin, 1966).

In working with cases of severe reading disability, it is
especially important to recognize their difficulty in abstraction
and/or in identifying letters in isolation, when they are printed
in another color, or in a different size. These individuals have
difficulty in transferring the characteristic quality of one Gestalt

to another configuration. They have difficulty in fusing sounds and integrating parts into wholes. When taught in shorter units, they "catch on" more easily. The dyslexic child, while responding to whole words and sentences, needs additional help in structuring and organizing them. A much closer relationship between clinical methods and findings and reading instruction is necessary first to understand the strengths and weaknesses of a particular child and then to learn how to help him learn.

Identification of severe cases

An informal and effective way of identifying organically-caused reading disability is to note otherwise normal children who do not learn to read in response to educational methods that are effective with the large majority. However, children with organic defects can often succeed with the pre-reading work of the first grade. "The learning block does not become manifest until actual reading begins" (Peck, Zwerling, Rabban, & Mendelsohn, 1966, p. 425). An indication of generalized verbal incapacity is a verbal I.Q. on the WISC twenty points lower than the performance I.Q. A reading-readiness test given to kindergarten children and first graders is useful as a screening device. Scores at the fiftieth percentile or lower call attention to a large proportion of children with possible learning problems and, in some instances, may also uncover otherwise unrecognized psychopathology in child and family (Peck, *et al.,* 1966, p. 432).

In studies of severe reading disability, a large number of tests have been used. The following battery was used in Leten's (1962) study:

Revised Stanford-Binet
Raven's Progressive Matrices
Bender Visual-Motor Gestalt
Benton Revised Visual Retention Test
Graham and Kendall Memory-for-Design Test

Jastak Wide-Range Achievement Test

Electro-oculogram recordings during oral and silent reading of a series of paragraphs

Developmental history

Minnesota Percepto-Diagnostic Test (MPD) (Krippner,
1966a)

The case-study approach based on minute investigation of
individual cases and on therapeutic experience and remedial
work contributes to the etiology, diagnosis, theoretical concepts, and treatment of these cases.

On the deepest level of diagnosis, hereditary, encephalo-
pathic, social, and psychological factors are all involved (Kucera, Matejcek, & Langmeier, 1963).

The complexity of causation of severe reading difficulty
makes diagnosis and research extremely difficult. If, as Peck
and his associates have said:

. . . disproportionately larger numbers of children with
neurologic damage, children from families of lower socio-
economic classes, or children in cultures which place lesser
emphasis upon education and upon planning for the future
are to be counted among the children with reading disability, then no study of this system can leave any of these variables uncontrolled. (Peck, *et al.,* 1966, p. 42)

Diagnostic study utilizing all available data seems essential for
long-range planning for these children(Silver & Hagin, 1966).

Treatment

The most important factor in treatment is the dy-
namic process that affects the whole person. The most pervasive
way to treat reading disability is to increase the individual's ego
strength, to strengthen the whole personality. But, other learning
conditions and methods are also essential. Cruickshank, Bentzen, Ratzeburg, and Tannhauser (1961) described four major
remedial procedures for brain-injured and hyperactive cases:
1] reduction of environmental space,   *2*] reduction of unessen-

tial visual and auditory stimuli,   3] establishment of a highly
structured program, and   4] increase of the stimulus value of
the instructional material.

Since many of these individuals are easily distracted, environmental distractions—pictures and other objects in their field
of vision, noises, jewelry worn by the worker, and the like—
should be eliminated as far as possible. The child needs to focus
on the thing to be learned. It is even helpful to cover the printed
page with an oak-tag sheet in which a slit exposes one word or
phrase or sentence at a time.

Since these cases have difficulty in organizing perception
and seeing configurations or words as wholes, a concept helpful
to them is of letters and clusters of letters as cars which must
be hitched together to make a word, or words similarly linked to
make sentences. It is:

> . . . economical to use both phonic and visual-recognition
> methods of teaching reading. When only the visual method
> is used, many children with competence in concept forma-
> tion evolve their own concepts of phonetic identities and
> constancies. When only the phonic method is used, it can-
> not apply to phonetically irregular words. Moreover, all
> reading vocabulary eventually becomes sight-recognition
> vocabulary for the accomplished, speedy reader. He ac-
> quires a vast inventory of words, each one of which is re-
> cognizable on sight, almost instantaneously. (Money, 1962,
> p. 25)

These individuals need special help in linking visual with auditory images of words and in organizing perceptions into concepts and concepts into patterns or "gestalten." Concepts can be
developed through oral language and reading. As the child acquires the ability to learn through the printed word, he also
acquires vocabulary and extends and broadens the concept-
formation process. Neurologically, if development follows use,
lack of development follows lack of use. Reading disability is a
"vital factor in intellectual and psychological maturation" (Wepman, 1962, p. 186). These individuals need special help to get
the central thought of a paragraph by beginning with very simple, well-constructed paragraphs and noting the contribution

which the topic sentence and each succeeding sentence make to the structure and purpose of the paragraph.

One point of view regarding remediation is that because of the lack of demonstrated relationship between behavioral characteristics and neurological findings, treatment must be non-specific and directed to utilizing the open or uninjured channels (Cohn, 1964).

Another view emphasizes strengthening areas of deficit. Actually, building on strengths and strengthening weak areas should go on almost simultaneously, first using the intact channels to build confidence and then giving practice and instruction to restore or develop defective abilities. For example, if auditory discrimination is good and visual discrimination is poor, first reading skills should be taught by a basically auditory approach (phonic and linguistic clues), and second, visual perceptual training should be given if the client seems to profit by it. When visual discrimination begins to function adequately, other approaches to word analysis such as use of context clues can be attempted. An individual approach to each client is needed.

Many specific methods and procedures that can be used in the classroom are described by Cruickshank, Bentzen, Ratzeburg, and Tannhauser (1961).

The Baltimore County Public Schools clinical program, described by Schiffman (1962), accepts clients who are able to comprehend material read to them, but who exhibit serious difficulty in reading. A complete reading analysis is made on the basis of developmental history, individual intelligence tests, personality assessments including the Rorschach and Draw-A-Person tests, standardized reading achievement tests, informal analysis of reading skills, Gates Associative Learning Test, Detroit Tests of Learning Aptitude (Baker & Leland, 1935-55), laterality tests, physical screening, Bender Visual Motor Gestalt Test (Bender, 1938-46), Frostig Test of Perceptual Development, and the Eisenson Examining for Aphasia. Of particular diagnostic value are the Word Recognition Test and the Informal Reading Inventory. The Word Recognition Test consists of a graded list of words which are first flashed to ascertain the pupil's sight vocabulary. If the pupil mispronounces a word, he may look at it as long as he needs to and, in this way, reveals his word-attack skills. The Informal Reading Inventory gives information about the pupil's reading levels and difficulties.

In the Baltimore County program, the elementary school child reports to the clinic at 9:00 each morning and stays until 11:40. He attends regular school at the clinic in the afternoon from 12:45 to 3:30. Parents are required to attend seven PTA meetings during the year and four other meetings conducted by a school social worker. The directed-reading approach with basal-reader material and the experience-related approach employing a combination of visual and auditory techniques, plus the Fernald method and the Gillingham synthetic approach, are all used. The principles underlying the procedures are: *1*] to begin with small units that the pupil can handle easily and proceed slowly to more complex sequential steps, and *2*] to use all sensory pathways.

A case study by Krippner (1966a) described methods of remediation in more detail. Krippner presented the case of Jim who was ten years old, of average intelligence, but who had suffered a childhood head injury. His comprehension, imagery, and recall were all poor, and his spelling was extremely deficient.

Several techniques were employed to overcome these problems. Jim was given practice in locating the main idea, after understanding first what was meant by "main idea." He studied the nature and function of maps, then applied this knowledge in map-reading lessons. His experience stories were related, recorded, listened to, and then written down, with a title appropriately selected. These stories made the connection between spoken and written language apparent. In addition, they gave practice in needed skills. Jim had to organize his thoughts into a logical sequence before writing the story and, after writing it, he checked his spelling, divided the story into paragraphs, rewrote it, and sometimes typed, outlined, or dramatized it.

Jim also used the Science Research Associates Reading for

Understanding Laboratory to help with his comprehension skills. The Radaker (1962) technique was useful in improving spelling. This technique requires the child to close his eyes, try to re-see the word he is studying, re-hear it, then imagine a screen on which the word appears.

These methods were later applied to books, and Jim was given the opportunity for self-selection.

At the end of the academic year, his oral reading was somewhat above grade level, comprehension was at grade level, and spelling had improved but was still below grade level.

When brain injury is suspected, visual-perceptual-motor training is emphasized. The child is helped to regulate and coordinate different parts of his body into meaningful movement. For example, he engages in games such as making believe he is a puppet and has to move his various joints into different positions, or a flower growing up from the ground, or a jack-in-the-box into which he has to fold himself and then jump out to a full-length position. He becomes familiar with movement through space, walking over puddles of different sizes and walking at different rates, e.g. walking to school and walking home after school to play ball.

If a child has developed these basic aspects of awareness and control of his body, he will be able to acquire the higher-level skills of skipping, jumping, climbing, hopping, and running. These pave the way to more complicated games such as "Loopy Lou," "In and Out the Window," and "Simon Says." He also learns to move rhythmically in response to music. Playground activities lead to writing and reading. The transition is made from these various games to visual-motor-directional exercises with a pencil such as in the Frostig training material. Throwing a bean bag into a small box or darts at a target is preparation for the eye-hand coordination needed in writing. Children may engage in many of these activities and games in the same period of time. These enjoyable activities also offer opportunity for informal diagnosis and training of visual-perceptual-motor abilities.

Follow-up of treatment

Results of treatment of many cases of severe reading disability, however, are likely to be discouraging. Gallagher (1960) is to be commended for his follow-up, control-group study of 21 brain-injured retarded children, given individual tutoring for two years. He found that verbal skills improved more than non-verbal skills and that eight to ten year olds improved more than did ten to twelve years olds. More progress is usually made with cases of less severe initial retardation and with those who show developmental rather than organic etiologies. When tutoring stopped, the children tended either to regress to their previous lower developmental levels or to make no further gains. The most significant drops in verbal I.Q. were in cases where the original gains had been the greatest. The maintenance of gains resulting from special teaching procedures apparently was dependent on continued remedial support. Severe reading disability is only temporarily improved, not permanently removed, by short-term intensive treatment. It is more like a chronic illness for which long-term, supportive treatment is required (Balow & Blomquist, 1965).

It may be that an individual's original growth curve cannot be deflected by special treatment. On the other hand, present knowledge of the functioning of the brain as a whole suggests the possibility of compensation even for injured areas. Moreover, there is the possibility of more effective instruction than has been given in the past, instruction that makes clients aware of the methods by which progress is achieved, that emphasizes the individual's responsibility for his own growth, and that provides for continuing motivation toward specific goals.

4. *Diagnostic techniques*

An understanding of the reading process (Strang, 1965c) and correlates of reading development and difficulties must be accompanied by ability to use various diagnostic techniques. From observation in the classroom to clinical and neurological study of individual cases, diagnostic techniques cover a wide range.

Some of these techniques have already been referred to in previous sections of this paper. All of them have been described in other sources; each would warrant a separate monograph devoted to an appraisal of the technique and its application in diagnosis. The purpose of this chapter is merely to call attention to the importance and use of various methods of obtaining diagnostic information and to refer to certain techniques that have recently been developed and recommended. There is almost a complete dearth of research on the diagnostic process and techniques *per se* except in the area of standardized tests.

Research, clinical and case studies, and surveys have reported a large number of characteristics and patterns of characteristics associated with reading development and disability. Poor readers seem to have acquired different response patterns than those of effective readers. The traditional diagnostic approaches have had a pathological emphasis. They have focused too exclusively on what an individual *cannot do* rather than on what he actually *does* under certain conditions. They have not recognized that a student may function more effectively under certain conditions than under others.

Observation

Teachers and clinicians should be "child watchers." They should have: *1*] a background knowledge of behavior and conditions frequently associated with reading achievement and difficulties; 2] techniques of accurate, insightful observation; and 3] ability to understand or interpret the behavior they have observed. Teachers can be taught to observe students in the classroom and thus obtain valuable diagnostic information that they often can immediately use.

Much valuable understanding of correlates of reading achievement can be obtained while teaching. For example, diagnosis of the skills of eye-hand coordination, visual and auditory memory, facility in the spoken language, and other prerequisites to success in learning to read can be made in the school setting. These behaviors are part of the child's daily work and play activities. Tape recordings of spontaneous conversation of children in groups yield valuable information on their vocabulary, sentence structure, and logical thinking. Signs of visual and auditory impairment are evident in the child's bodily postures, his apparent discomfort in reading, his superior performance in spelling when the teacher stands close to him. Most useful is observation and analysis of the setting in which children experience success or failure in various reading tasks.

With training in methods of direct unstructured observation, teachers in 48 kindergarten classes learned to observe the characteristics of each child in their classes. By means of a scale of performance items, the teachers collected additional information on behavior such as visual and auditory perception and discrimination. On the basis of their observation, they identified one-quarter of their children whom they considered to be "high risks in the probability of developing learning problems" (Haring & Ridgway, 1967, p. 389). The investigators also administered the Stanford-Binet and three sub-tests of the WISC, as well as eight other diagnostic instruments to those children whom the teachers had identified as "poor risks." Haring and Ridgway concluded that the teacher plays a key role in the early identification of children with learning disabilities and that even a battery of tests does not predict as effectively as teacher observation of the individual child. They said:

An adequate basis for preventive and/or remedial teaching is provided by an ongoing analysis of classroom behavior, with emphasis on the skill performance and language-related variables as they involve classroom learning tasks. (1967, p. 393)

Lytton (1961) likewise conducted an experiment to determine whether the selection of pupils for special remedial work based on discrepancy between the mental age and the reading age was a better predictor of "adjustment success" than teachers' subjective assessment of the child's intelligence. The teachers were asked to balance the child's degree of backwardness against his likely "adjustability." Lytton (1961, p. 87) said that "the children whom the teachers chose did quite as well in reading as those selected by tests . . . although the average I.Q. of teacher-selected children was lower than that of test-selected children."

These two studies suggest that day-by-day observation by trained teachers who respond immediately to the strengths and difficulties they observe in children's reading may be as effective and far more practical than elaborate test batteries. As teachers incorporate principles and procedures of effective diagnosis and remedial work into their daily classroom teaching, the distinction between classroom teaching and remedial teaching will diminish.

The limitations of observation must also be recognized. Although the individual kindergarten teacher's assessment of the child is often remarkably accurate, it represents a subjective judgment. Moreover, "not all teachers possess the training, intuition, or experience that would enable them to make a reliable evaluation of a child's readiness" (de Hirsch, Jansky, & Langford, 1966, p. 3).

It is also true that what one sees is influenced by what one has in mind. Observations may be influenced by the observer's beliefs and biases about reading development, his interest in the children observed, and even by a subtle expectancy of a child's success or failure. This tendency emphasizes the importance of understanding the reading process and common causes of reading difficulty and of being receptive to what the child is trying to say through his behavior.

Diagnosis through tests

Reference to certain tests has already been made in
connection with specific reading abilities. More detail is given in
other published sources such as Bond and Tinker's *Reading
Difficulties, Their Diagnosis and Treatment* (1967, Chaps. 8,
9); Strang, McCullough, and Traxler's *The Improvement of
Reading* (1967, Chaps. 4, 5); Money's *The Disabled Reader*
(1966, pp. 402-07); and the latest edition of *Mental Measurement Yearbook* (Buros, 1965). In this chapter, only a few general comments on various tests and reports on some special research studies are included.

When making a diagnosis, the reading teacher or psychologist chooses a variety of tests, each of which gives additional information about the clients. If the tests overlap, there is a loss of
time and efficiency. Therefore, facts on the amount of duplica-
tion in different tests given to the same subjects is useful information for the diagnostician. For example, in 1941 Traxler concluded that the Van Wagenen-Dvorak Diagnostic Examination
of Silent Reading Abilities did not really measure the separate
abilities designated. Most of the parts were so highly correlated
that diagnosis based on the sub-scores contributed little to an
understanding of the individual's specific difficulties. Many other
studies of a large number of reading abilities, using factor analysis, agree that most of the measurable variance in tests of reading competence can be accounted for by a fairly small number
of factors (Lennon, 1962). Although, as Holmes (1961)
pointed out in his substrata study, improvement in one ability
results in increased proficiency in a number of related abilities.

The most valuable measures of reading achievement give
information about specific reading skills as well as a global total
score. They include open-ended or creative response as well as
multiple-choice items, and they analyze responses qualitatively
instead of merely as right and wrong.

Criticisms, such as the following, have been made of the
interpretation and use of standardized tests:

The tests used are of little diagnostic value.

The interpretation of test results is often superficial and
sometimes faulty.

Tests are often given without a clearly defined purpose. Much valuable diagnostic information is never extracted from tests.

The diagnostic information available on tests is often not used directly in helping students improve their reading.

Too little attention is given to the conditions under which the test is administered.

In the interpretation of test results, the influence of factors that may affect test performance should be considered. McDonald (1960) obtained experimental evidence that reading comprehension is significantly impaired by periodic interruptions such as writing the elapsed time on the chalkboard every minute. This detrimental effect was especially evident in students rated as highly anxious. The length of the reading passage did not seem to affect reading performance. In re-testing, practice effort is obviously present; the increase in scores after one month cannot be attributed entirely to maturation. Curr and Gourlay (1960, p. 159) found the practice effect in the Schonell test to be "about twice as great for the Reading Comprehension Test as for the Graded Word Reading Test." Differences in standardization of the forms of the test as well as factors other than practice *per se* influence the re-test results.

Often personality factors that may influence an individual's test results are not taken into account. Emotional factors affect reading performance in devious ways. Stress and anxiety, need for achievement, responsive styles—acquiescence, overgeneralizations, tendency to give socially approved responses, and impulsivity. Despite the efforts of test constructors, these extraneous factors influence test performance and, consequently, the predictability of tests. In a study of 101 college students, Rankin (1963) found a relationship between introversion-extroversion and reading-test reliability and validity:

The greater the degree of extroversion, the smaller the reliability and validity appear to be. Therefore, greater confidence can be placed in predictability of reading test results for introverts than for extroverts. (Rankin, 1963, p. 116)

There is a danger of relying too much on the grade scores obtained from standardized tests. These scores show the level at which comprehension can be achieved with difficulty rather than the level at which fluency and reasonable accuracy can be expected. Therefore, especially with children who already feel a keen sense of failure, it is wise to give them reading material one or two years below the level indicated by test scores. Starting at an easy level can do little harm; starting at too high a level may shatter a child's dawning interest and hope of improvement.

The effect on an individual of knowledge of his test results is often ignored. To learn where one stands on a reading test stimulates some students and makes them receptive to needed instruction and practice. But to a sensitive, easily discouraged child, a low score on a standardized test confirms his sense of failure.

Standardized tests themselves have limitations that should be more clearly recognized:

1] Some tests overestimate pupils' reading ability. For example, the Gates Advanced Primary Reading Test tends to overestimate reading level by approximately two years (Leibert, 1965).

2] Other tests show gains or losses in reading ability after a period of remedial instruction, depending upon which form of the test is given first. "Comparable" forms of the same test are assumed to be parallel but often are not.

3] Still other tests are highly influenced by the speed at which the student works.

4] Some tests lose validity at different age levels. For example, if a student's reading level is below the sixth grade, the California Test of Mental Maturity scores may not be valid.

5] Guessing may unduly raise scores on many standardized tests.

6] Interpretation of scores may be misleading if the population tested is different from that on which the test norms were based.

7] For some groups, the test ceiling is too low. In other words, the test is not sufficiently powerful for the particular sample of students.

8] Many research results are based on single scores which have limited validity. Cumulative results, seldom reported, become progressively more dependable.

9] Changes in revisions of tests are often not taken into consideration.

10] The grade level estimated by the test may be higher than the grade level of books the student can actually read.

11] Tests do not always correlate with performance. An individual's performance may fluctuate on a particular day.

12] The tests sample a limited number of reading abilities: They do not measure the ability to "disentangle concepts from context." They do not provide a measure of ability to evaluate in depth or to support a choice. They cannot measure subtle, individual aspects of appreciation of literature or creative reading. They generally do not measure ability to communicate ideas or concepts to others; multiple-choice tests measure merely the ability to recognize the most plausible of four or five responses.

Awareness of these limitations helps to prevent many errors in diagnostic formulations.

Although the informal reading inventories have many obvious advantages, most reading teachers seem to feel more secure when using standardized tests. McCracken (1962) compared the grade-level ratings of a group of sixth-grade children on the Iowa Test of Basic Skills, Form I, with ratings obtained on an informal reading inventory. The average difference between the Iowa reading-comprehension grade levels and the informal, immediate, instructional-reading levels was 2.3 years; the correlation was .78. The difference in some individual cases was from three to five years. The Iowa test rated most of the children higher in both comprehension and vocabulary than did the informal inventory. A book on the grade level indicated by the standardized test would actually be on the child's frustration level.

The informal inventory is more valuable as a self-appraisal teaching device than as a testing technique. It lends itself to self-diagnosis based on a profile which each student constructs and uses to make an individual plan for self-instruction and practice.

Tests of prerequisites to reading
TESTS OF VISUAL-MOTOR PERCEPTION

The interest in early diagnosis of reading disability is reflected in the references on various tests of visual-motor abilities. Some of the most widely used or the most recently developed are briefly described here.

Bender-Gestalt tests. Probably the oldest and most widely used test in this category is the Bender Visual-Motor Gestalt Test, often referred to as the Bender-Gestalt:

Visual-Motor Gestalt Test (Bender, 1946)

The Bender Gestalt Test (Pascal & Suttell, 1951)

Revised Bender Gestalt Test (Hutt & Briskin, 1960)

The Bender Visual Motor Gestalt Test for Children (Clawson, 1962)

The Bender Gestalt Test for Young Children (Koppitz, 1964)

The Visual Motor Gestalt Test Two-Copy Drawing Form (Western Psychological Services, 1964)

This test and an experiment using the test in relation to reading achievement are well described in an article by Leton (1962). He found that "reading disability cases, and particularly those with perceptual retardation, were more deficient in grapho-motor skills than were normal readers" (1962, p. 429). The case studies Leton reported, in which he reproduced a Bender-Gestalt profile for a good reader and for one who is emotionally disturbed, are valuable to the clinician for comparison with his own results. The description of a comprehensive clinical procedure and the electro-oculogram tracings for the control group, the emotionally disturbed, and the perceptually handicapped readers are also useful in interpreting individual cases. The search for an instrument that would early identify potential reading problems, provide a basis for optimal placement of children in a beginning reading program, and predict later reading achievement led to studies of the Bender Visual Motor Gestalt Test as a screening instrument for this purpose.

Two group methods of administering the test—one using a test booklet with a single design reproduced at the top of each page, and another method in which the children copy on blank pages the designs presented to them on cards—compared favorably with the standard method of administration (Carol E. Smith & Keogh, 1962).

A later study by Keogh (1965), using the group Bender Visual Motor Gestalt Test and two methods of scoring, reported that the best prediction of third-grade achievement was from the total score. Although the Bender reflected a general pattern of school performance, poor scores were not predictive of third-grade reading achievement. However, when administered to 272 children at the beginning of the first grade, it predicted total average achievement, as measured by the Metropolitan Achievement Test, as well as the Lee-Clark and Metropolitan Readiness tests. The Lee-Clark tends to overestimate achievement, whereas the Bender and the Metropolitan Readiness Test tend to underestimate achievement more often. The Lee-Clark appears to be "more strongly influenced by cultural and social factors, while the Bender reveals apparently more the potential ability in visual-motor perception" (Kopitz, Mardis, & Stephens, 1961, p. 81).

Attainment of certain levels on the Bender was associated with maturity in areas of development pertinent to reading; children who achieved well on the Bender were apt to achieve well in other aspects of the school program. . . . The group Bender is of limited validity for prediction and diagnosis of individual cases of reading disability at primary grades, but it warrants consideration as a possible screening technique for early identification of children likely to be successful in the school program. (Keogh, 1965, p. 84)

The Bender Visual Motor Gestalt compares favorably with certain readiness tests as a predictor of first-grade achievement. It may be of most value in kindergarten and first grade in identifying development of visual-motor abilities that may be associated with reading readiness. It does not yield the kind of diagnostic information teachers can use to help a child gain proficiency in abilities in which he is weak. For this purpose, teachers' skillful observation can be more effective in leading immediately to remediation with an individual child or a group.

The Perceptual Forms Test (1963).   This is a visual-perception and visual-memory test for children ages 6.0 to 8.5. It utilizes seven basic designs described by Gesell—circle, cross, square, triangle, rectangle, and diamond, oriented horizontally and vertically. The child draws one form at a time. The drawing of the forms is followed by a series of incomplete forms to test the children's memory for the designs just completed. The test was originally designed to measure hand-eye coordination. According to the test manual, a child who scores more than 60 can be expected to possess "a sensory-motor-perception pattern adequate for tasks related to beginning school learning." Since the test does not appear to be very effective at the age of eight, an extension of its age range and an effort to increase its accuracy of discrimination have been suggested. To increase its predictive value, the replacement of the cross and square by two more difficult items seems advisable.

Marianne Frostig Developmental Test of Visual Perception

(Frostig, Lefever, & Whittlesey, 1964). On the basis of observation in the clinic, Frostig noted the children's poor eye-hand coordination in writing; their inability to recognize words, particularly a word or letter in a different size or style of type than the one first seen; their reversals, rotations, mirror writing, and tendency to interchange letters within a word. This observation was the basis for developing five tests of visual perception: 1] eye-hand coordination, 2] figure-ground perception, 3] form constancy, 4] perception of position in space, and 5] spatial relationships. Factor analysis showed that two major factors accounted for most of the variance: general intelligence and developmental changes in perception.

Frostig first studied the results of the test with normal children, then discovered ways in which exceptional children were different (Frostig, Lefever, & Whittlesey, 1961). There have been three editions (Maslow, Frostig, Lefever, & Whittlesey, 1964; Frostig, Lefever, & Whittlesey, 1961). The test was standardized on 2,116 nursery school and public school children in Southern California. In this sample there were no Negro children; the majority were middle class. Perceptual ages and perceptual quotients were defined and scale scores developed.

The directions for administering and scoring the test are quite clear, although there are several instances of inappropriateness of vocabulary, such as "tunnel," for young children. The perceptual quotient needs to be more fully explained, and information for evaluating the test is incomplete. The re-test reliability was reported as .98, .80, .29 to .74 with different population samples; the split-half reliability as .78-.89. The correlations of the test results with motor coordination, intelligence, and classroom adjustment as rated by teachers, was around .50. The correlations between classroom adjustment and the Frostig Test of Visual Perception decreased markedly with age: kindergarten, .51; grade one, .43; grade two, .28; and grade three, .08. (Frostig, et al., 1961). Of the reading problems in kindergarten with perceptual quotients below 90, seventy per cent fell below the midpoint in reading achievement. The test identifies many children who would not attempt to learn to read or who had severe reading difficulties. Other studies indicate that the test has little use beyond the first grade.

Any kind of maladjustment tends to show up in respect to functions that represent the major developmental task for a given age. Neurologically handicapped children also scored much lower than the average on the Frostig test. A later study by Olson (1966) reported that the Frostig test did not predict specific reading difficulty in the case of second-grade children. The Frostig scores showed a small degree of relationship with specific reading abilities, mental age, and chronological age.

A more valuable feature is the diagnostic aspect and the training program, consisting of worksheets for each of the five areas. These enable the teacher to give children specific practice in abilities in which the test showed them to be weak and thus build a good foundation for beginning reading in the first grade.

Minnesota Percepto-Diagnostic Test (Fuller & Laird, 1963). The Minnesota Percepto-Diagnostic Test (MPD) is a test of directional orientation. This is a rapid and objective method designed to distinguish organic, primary, and secondary reading disability. The test consists of six Gestalt designs to be copied. The only scoring criterion is degrees of rotation of the copied figure away from the orientation of the original. The MPD was administered to two groups of boys eight to fifteen years of age, with a mean I.Q. of 111.5. The reading-disability group rotated the figures 11.56°; the good readers, 1.86°. The difference was highly significant. Using Rabinovitch's (1959) classification with a larger number of children, Fuller and Laird found that 85 to 100 per cent of children having primary, secondary, or organic reading difficulties were correctly identified by this test. In using the test, the examiner must decide whether the case is primarily a reading disability or an emotional problem. The degree of rotation which is said to indicate organic reading disability is larger for the behavioral problems than for those with reading disability only.

PREDICTIVE INDEXES

de Hirsch Predictive Index.   To date, the most comprehensive study designed to predict reading readiness and problems was reported by de Hirsch, Jansky, and Langford (1966). Their tests explore many facets of perceptuo-motor and oral-language organization. Initially 37 "tests" were administered, covering specific prerequisites to success in beginning reading. Immediately after testing in the kindergarten, a profile that supplemented the statistical data with clinical observations was made, summarizing each child's over-all functioning. At the end of the first grade, the children were given a writing test. Among the 37 tests, 19 were significantly related to reading performance, 20 to spelling, and 16 to writing. The Predictive Index that was finally developed consisted of ten tests (de Hirsch, *et al.*, 1966, pp. 41-42):

Pencil use
Bender Visual-Motor Gestalt
Wepman Auditory Discrimination Test
Number of words used in their dictated story
Categories, general names for three clusters of words
Horst Reversal Test
Gates Word Matching Test
Word Recognition I and II
Word Reproduction

The types of difficulty most common to the largest number of failing readers were, in order of frequency: reversals, auditory discrimination, categorization, Bender Visual-Motor Gestalt tasks, word recognition, and human-figure drawing. I.Q. ranked lower than these as a predictor of reading achievement. This prognostic battery was successful in identifying children of kindergarten age who were high risks for later achievement in reading, spelling, and writing.

Whether or not teachers use the de Hirsch battery, they should be alert to the kinds of perceptual-motor and oral-language skills that seemed to be most closely related to failure in reading. For children showing these deficiencies, informal and enjoyable reading-readiness exercises should be given.

Wepman battery (in process).   A still more comprehensive battery of tests to diagnose and predict reading readiness and achievement is one being developed by Wepman and his associates (in process). To his Auditory Discrimination Test will be added a Visual Discrimination Test and other instruments for assessing factors related to success in reading. The Chicago Visual Discrimination Test by Wepman and his associates (University of Chicago Press, 1967) is part of this new battery to measure children's perceptual and conceptual abilities.

The Illinois Test of Psycholinguistic Abilities, Experimental Edition (McCarthy & Kirk, 1961-63). Deeper levels of diagnosis require the study of psychological as well as perceptual reading achievement. An important diagnostic instrument combining perceptual, linguistic, and cognitive factors is the Illinois Test of Psycholinguistic Abilities (ITPA) (Kirk & McCarthy, 1961). This test attempts to diagnose the reading process from intake to output through the stages of decoding, associative mental processing, and encoding on both the representational and automatic sequential levels. It is a unique approach to differential diagnosis of the reading process, based on a profile analysis. More than a decade of careful work is represented in the present form, and work on a revised ITPA is under way to increase both reliability and validity. More than fifty studies have already been made on the relationship among sub-scales and between sub-scale performance and reading behavior. The relationships between ITPA and other correlates of reading achievement have also been studied. For example, recognizing that the ITPA was incomplete, Kass (1966) supplemented it with: *1*] tests of visual closure measuring ability to predict the whole from a part, to guess what the completed picture will be;   *2*] sound-blending test of ability to tell what word a series of separate sounds make;   *3*] maze test which seems to involve a "visual-motor predictive process and may bear some relation to eye-hand coordination" (Kass, 1966, p. 534);   *4*] memory-for-design test to assess the ability to reproduce from

memory simple geometric designs; and 5] perceptual speed
test of ability to discriminate details that differentiate words.

Children with reading disability were deficient in the above
abilities, especially at the integrative level. Brain damage may
affect the integrational functions such as closure, sequential memory, and rate of recognition. Children who have difficulty in
handling the symbols in reading may compensate by getting information from pictures. Reading represents an integration of
many skills.

Visual-motor aspects of other tests.   Reading-readiness tests
have at least one sub-test of visual perception. The Monroe
Reading Aptitude Test, Primary Form (Monroe, 1935), has an
excellent visual-perception and visual-memory test and one for
other aspects of visual memory. The Harrison-Stroud Reading
Readiness Profiles (Harrison & Stroud, 1949-56), The Gates
Reading Readiness Tests (Gates, 1942), and the Lee-Clark
Reading Readiness Test (Lee & Clark, 1962) also include
measures of visual perception.

Intelligence tests, too, have sub-tests which involve visual
perception. The Wechsler Primary and Pre-school Scale of Intelligence (WPPSI) (Wechsler, 1966) includes one test of copying geometric designs. The WISC has several tests involving
visual perception as well as visual-motor coordination. Visual-
perception tasks are also included in the Stanford-Binet, the
Columbia Mental Maturity Scale, the Merrill-Palmer, and the
Arthur Performance Scale.

A BATTERY FOR DIAGNOSIS OF BEGINNING READING

An individual testing sequence to diagnosis, prerequisite to
beginning reading, might include the following:

The Wide-Range Achievement Test
An individual reading inventory
The Wepman Test of Auditory Discrimination
The Frostig Test of Visual Perception
The Illinois Test of Psycholinguistic Abilities

A sequence to diagnose basic reading skills—word recognition, word attack, literal comprehension—might be the following:

An informal individual reading inventory
The Dolch Basic Sight Vocabulary Test
The McCullough Word Analysis Tests
The Metropolitan Reading Readiness Tests

THE CLOZE TECHNIQUE

The name of this technique suggests the Gestalt psychology concept of closure. Certain words are systematically omitted in a passage, and the students are instructed to fill each blank with the missing word. The most common procedure is to select randomly one of the first words in the passage and then follow this selection with the deletion of every fifth or tenth word. To ascertain the effect of deletion of certain grammatical categories (nouns, verbs, modifiers, prepositions, conjunctions, and noun determiners), each of these syntactical units is systematically deleted in the same way.

The cloze procedure has been used in several ways: as a measure of readability, and of reading comprehension, and as a teaching device. Bormuth (1964) presented it as a new method of measuring the grammatical complexity of sentences. The relationship of results on cloze techniques to reading achievement has been demonstrated. Bormuth (1967) reported that a person who correctly answered 38 per cent of the cloze items usually obtained a multiple-choice raw score of 90 per cent. In some instances, the correlations have been higher than these with intelligence-test scores. Sixth-grade pupils increased in vocabulary and comprehension but not in speed as a result of practice on two types of cloze practice exercises. However, those "who had completed the cloze exercises did not show significantly greater improvement in reading comprehension than the control group" (Schneyer, 1965, p. 176).

The cloze procedure may be self-reinforcing. Or, it may be motivated by reinforcement of the correct response by the teacher and by objective evidence of progress in a series of exercises.

Schneyer (1965) asked teachers to score students' papers for the precise word used by the author and to return the papers to the students the next day. In this procedure, the students might feel frustrated rather than receive reinforcement if the word they had inserted was appropriate, even though it was not the precise word used in the original passage. In the Bloomer (1962) study, the subjects graded the papers themselves, then turned in their papers to be graded by the instructor for correct meaning. Thus, any frustration resulting from not having inserted the word the author used would be neutralized by the instructor's approval of their having recognized one correct meaning.

Although the ability to make closures appears to be related to reading ability, the effect on comprehension depends upon the type of cloze-procedure exercise. Noun deletions seem to offer more clues to comprehension than modifier deletions which tend to distort the meaning of the passage and make comprehension of the passage more difficult.

The child learns that certain sequences tend to recur and that certain words convey more information than others. This principle is shown clearly by the cloze technique. When certain words are left out, the poor readers have difficulty in guessing what the words might be. Familiarity with book language gives the reader clues from the context and from the syntax of the sentence. Structural linguists emphasize this. When a reader gives inappropriate responses, his difficulty may be partly due to the content and context of the reading material.

The cloze technique, scored as a number of correct word insertions, can be used to throw light on an individual's ability to use context clues and on his understanding of syntax-position of words in sentences (Cromer & Weiner, 1966).

Notes on tests of certain aspects of reading achievement*

A vocabulary test of the open-end type like that of the Stanford-Binet or Wechsler intelligence test yields information as to the depth and types of comprehension of words in isolation. Poor readers tend to give less generalized responses on such a vocabulary test; they are more likely to give idiosyncratic or personal responses.

Individual testing of oral reading is useful to assess word-recognition skills, basic sight vocabulary, and expression, phrasing, and articulation. It may also suggest the individual's attitudes toward reading and toward himself. Such an appraisal is essential to an understanding of the process of learning to read. In addition to noting the frequency of the different kinds of errors made, the examiner may also encourage the individual to describe the method of word attack by which he arrived at a correct or incorrect pronunciation.

Measures of speed of reading leave much to be desired. Since speed is meaningless apart from comprehension, it should be measured as an integral part of comprehension, as in the Cooperative Reading Tests and the Davis Reading Tests (Davis & Davis, 1956-62). Another possibility is to measure the number of words read within a limited time set by the examiner as in the Iowa Silent Reading Tests. The most useful diagnostic information would be obtained informally by timing the individual's reading of different passages for different purposes and checking his comprehension as appropriate for each passage.

To determine the relationship of intelligence, perceptual speed, and closure to reading-rate improvement, Geake (1963) gave sixty students in grades seven through twelve the following tests before and immediately after thirty-two sessions of training in rapid reading:

Diagnostic Reading Tests, Survey Section
Stanford-Binet or WISC

---

*For a review and appraisal of reading tests, see Buros (1965) and Strang, McCullough, and Traxler (1967, Chap. 5).

Clerical Speed and Accuracy Test of the Differential Aptitude Test

Perceptual closure as measured by Thurstone's Mutilated Words Test

The students were grouped according to intelligence and initial reading rate. They were given verbal instruction to read as fast as possible, and their practice was supervised. Both fast and slow groups increased in rate, but lost in comprehension. Fifteen weeks after the end of instruction, there was a considerable loss in rate; but comprehension had returned to pre-experimental levels. Initially rapid readers made the greatest gains and maintained them better than the initially slow readers. The clozure test correlated significantly with rate gains. In remedial work with slow readers, further diagnosis of the causes of their slow reading should be made. In any attempt to increase speed of reading, two things should be stressed—speed of comprehension and flexibility and adjustment of rate to the reader's purpose and the kind of selection.

ELECTROENCEPHALOGRAM

A review of studies of EEG abnormality in dyslexia showed much variation among the different investigations with reference to the reading diagnostic value of this instrument (Benton & Bird, 1963). In one of the studies among 47 cases of behavior disorders reviewed by Benton and Bird, 34 of whom were also dyslexic, a high incidence (75 to 88 per cent) of EEG abnormality was found. In another study of 50 dyslexic children with case histories suggestive of brain damage, only 28 per cent EEG abnormality was detected. Over half (58 per cent) of a group of 41 children with speech retardation, dyslexia, or both, and obvious neurological, emotional, or intellectual disturbances had abnormal EEG records; but a group of children who were not conduct problems did not differ from the disturbed group in their EEG results. In general, research tends to show a higher than expected incidence of EEG abnormality in dyslexic children but

also wide variation, due partly to the diversity of the populations sampled and to the employment of different criteria of EEG
abnormality. From their review of studies, Benton and Bird
concluded that although dyslexic children with EEG abnormality
show other neurological, motor, visuo-perceptive, visuo-motor,
and speech disturbances, a "specific association between EEG
and reading disability has not been unequivocally demonstrated" (1963, p. 531).

Ratings, questionnaires, and interviews

Rating scales are useful as a guide to observation and
as a summary of observation. For example, statistically significant differences were found to exist between poor and good
readers on teachers' ratings of a number of personality variables
such as self-confidence, social attitude (ability to make contacts),
persistence, ability to concentrate, dominance-submissiveness,
emotional stability. A five-point scale included a range from an
unusual or exceptional degree to an extremely low degree of
the trait (Malmquist, 1960, p. 190).

Questionnaires are a generally unsatisfactory way of obtaining diagnostic information. The individual may not understand the question; he may not have the information asked; he
may unconsciously or consciously try to present himself in the
most favorable light; or he may resent the questions being
asked. Recently the possible detrimental effect of certain psychological and mental hygiene inventories has been considered.

If questions are asked in an interview situation, the interviewer has the opportunity to correct misconceptions and to
clarify his interpretation of the answers by further questioning.
Some kinds of data can be obtained more reliably than others.
Interview questionnaires which obtained information from parents on size of family, age, sex, and education of its members,
and facts about the living conditions can be considered highly
reliable. But, data on conditions of birth, the child's personality,

growth, speech defects during pre-school years, illnesses, and nervous traits are less reliably reported.

In the personal interview, the aim is not just to get information but to help the individual understand himself and his reading development and problems. The interview session itself offers opportunity for the client to learn to take initiative, to make decisions, to relate himself to another person, or to develop other ways of behaving that would contribute to his development as a whole person. The interview is also the most personalized way in which to give reading instruction.

The case study

The value of the case-study approach lies in the synthesis of information about an individual child. Very often one or more central factors become evident from which stem much of the observed behavior. This complex relationship among personal and environmental factors enables the worker to get to the root of the problem instead of merely treating surface behavior.

5. Problem of diagnosis in special groups

Diagnosis in pre-school and kindergarten

Special emphasis is being placed upon early diagnosis of characteristics and conditions that may facilitate or inhibit a child's reading development. During kindergarten years, certain aspects of child development necessary for success in learning to read should be assessed: physical development and impairments; large muscle coordination; eye-hand coordination; visual perception, discrimination, and memory; auditory perception, discrimination, and memory; visual attention span; directionality; auditory attention span; and general over-all language development. Research on each of these factors was brieflly reviewed by Haring and Ridgway (1967). There is evidence of the relationship of each of these factors to reading disabilities.

The diagnosis of possible brain damage should always include information on delivery and possible birth injuries. Unfortunately, parents' reports are not highly reliable. Medical reports are more accurate. The relation of premature birth to reading development has been reported as follows:

	Cases	Per cent*	Boys	Girls
Poor readers	11	20.8	10	1
Medium readers	25	8.7	15	10
Good readers	7	11.7	5	2

* Significant at the 5 per cent level.

From his investigation of this problem, Malmquist concluded that "poor readers tend to be born prematurely to a greater extent than do good readers" (1960, pp. 229-31).

The relation of reading development to weight at birth was not statistically significant, but the number of poor readers whose weight at birth was especially low has been found to be significantly greater than the number of good readers (5 per cent level).

Although the relation between reading and speech defects has not been clearly established, more boys than girls who are poor readers have been reported as having difficulties in speech.

The relationship between reading difficulties and physical diseases in general has not been established as statistically significant, but it is reasonable to suppose that anything that would lower the child's energy level, or divert his attention from intellectual development, or result in feelings of inadequacy, or deprive him of growth experiences would affect his development in reading.

On the pre-school level, predictive batteries and specific diagnostic tests which lead to remedial procedures have been and are being developed (Bateman, 1966). Representative is the prognostic test battery by de Hirsch, Jansky, and Langford (1966) which has been described in the previous chapter. It is designed to identify kindergarten-age children who are likely to fail later in reading, spelling, and writing. About one-half of this battery containing 37 tests of perceptomotor and linguistic development correlated significantly with second-grade achievement. Girls made better scores than boys on a large majority of these tests, but their reading achievement at the end of the second grade was not significantly superior. The ten tests finally included in the de Hirsch Predictive Index identified ten of the eleven disabled readers or spellers, but also singled out two who were adequate readers or spellers.

The data suggest the possibility of over-referrals. There are children who show psychological test performances characteristic of children with learning problems, yet they do not have reading difficulties. There may be a substantial number of these (Bateman, 1966). In the clinical observation of eight of the most severely deficient readers or spellers, five were shown to be unusually small, markedly hyperactive, distractible, impulsive, disinhibited, and infantile in their behavior. Some also showed severe graphomotor difficulties, crude human figure drawings, inferior auditory perception and oral language development. For these cases, special education preparatory to beginning reading was advocated.

Many methods of teaching pre-school children to read have been described. Most of the reports are of bright children taught through play-game activities. However, Fowler (1965) pointed out that both O. K. Moore and Montessori tended to discount the play approach in favor of manipulative activity and free choice in a planned and responsive environment. They also rejected or minimized "the role of praise and warmth evolving through the development of relationships with a teacher" (Fowler, 1965, p. 7). Further research is needed on problems of the relative effectiveness of various techniques and the possible harmful consequences of early reading instruction.

In an intensive study of three-year-old twins' and triplets' process of learning to read, Fowler (1965) was concerned with such questions as:

What level of competence in reading has been obtained for pre-school children?

At what age? At what ability level?

In what span of time?

With what rate or intensity of stimulation?

By what reading methods and what teaching techniques?

With what motivational or emotional consequences?

From his study of methods of presenting vocabulary and of conditions that affect motivation, Fowler (1965) concluded that many three-year-old children experience little difficulty in learning to read if they have a mental age of four years; three of the four three-year-old children with mental ages of four years learned to read fluently over a five-month period; they learned to read first-grade-level primers. The two rapid learners read well in only two months. They grasped relationships, that is, "phonic-letter units in relation to whole-word structures and especially word units in sentence-form patterning" (Fowler, 1965, p. 80). The two children whose mental age was less than three years made little progress in reading; they could not read a single sentence. They failed to apprehend the patternings of relationships. In brief, the bright children learned to read; the others did not. The bright children conceptualized "essential dimensions of word and sentence structure"(Fowler, 1965, p. 87); they grasped key concepts. The others remained on an individual unit perceptual-learning level. The children showed no signs of socio-emotional difficulty; some made gains in this aspect. In this study, emotional ups and downs came more often from home than from the experimental situation; often the child's initial mood improved as a result of participation and achievement in the games and in a rewarding relationship.

Nursery school is a place to build up all the skills that children from ideal homes usually have acquired by the time they come to school. If they have not learned to color between lines, cut with scissors, skip and hop, walk a balance board, speak correctly, now is the time to learn. For these children such manipulative and motor activities are not busywork. To develop tactuality, they can learn to distinguish objects by feeling them behind a screen or in a closed bag. To develop visual discrimination and retention, they can sort things of different colors, form, content; detect missing elements; and the like. Language usage and auditory recognition and retention can be checked through experiences such as talking on a phone, beating a drum, playing "Simon Says." Many interesting activities of this kind develop basic abilities needed for beginning reading and also contribute to the development of deeper levels of memory, concentration, conceptualization, and cognition.

The value of early diagnosis and treatment is emphasized by research as well as by experience. Schiffman (1964) reported that, on the basis of a four-year survey involving 10,000 children, when pupils with reading problems were identified by the second grade, they had a ten-times greater chance for successful remediation than did those identified at ninth grade. Moreover, many pupils in remedial classes failed to make progress when they returned to the regular program. These results might be different if more effective methods and instructional materials had been developed for the older children and if the transition from work in the remedial reading group to the classroom had been made more skillfully. Although in work with older retarded readers the weight of accumulated failure, nega-

tive self-concepts, increased complexity of the tasks, and established habits of perceiving and thinking make progress difficult,
they may have increased motivation through recognition of the
personal importance of reading. They may also have attained a
higher mental level. But the possibility still remains that if all
kindergarten children were screened with reference to these
prerequisites for success in reading and if they were placed in
an appropriate program, many later reading difficulties might be
prevented or overcome. A combination of favorable family
background, personality and skill of the teacher, and the quality
of kindergarten and classroom experience are crucial for early
school achievement in reading (Charlotte Silverman, 1967).

Formal reading instruction in the kindergarten has been
found to result in better reading achievement in the primary
grades, provided the teachers make provision for those children
who have learned to read before they enter school (Brzeinski,
1964). In another experiment with 221 kindergarten children
(Kelley & Chen, 1967), the superiority of the more formal instruction over the readiness program was evident for children of
both high and low intelligence. However, some of the low I.Q.
group fared better under readiness instruction. The children initially high in intelligence and readiness had better reading habits
and better attitudes toward school, regardless of the type of instruction.

Diagnosis of potential dropouts

Considerable research has been done on identifying
potential dropouts. In the potential dropout syndrome, reading
disability looms large. Many students drop out of high school
because of reading inability. Penty (1956) obtained clear evidence from data in the Battle Creek, Michigan school system
that the preponderance of early school-leavers stood in the lowest quarter with respect to reading ability; only 14.5 per cent of
those in the highest quarter left school before completing the
senior year. More than three times as many poor readers as

good readers dropped out of school. The poor readers who left school and those who remained to graduate had potential reading ability. With effective instruction they could have improved. Those who dropped out tended to be more irresponsible, impulsive, and less popular with classmates. Their school attendance was poor. They were often of low socio-economic status and had parents who had dropped out of school.

A study of potential dropouts among good and poor readers in the sixth grade (Watson, 1964) focused on the diagnosis of nine factors: socio-economic status, school absence, family mobility, age of starting to school, home stability, number of siblings, academic success, sex, and intelligence. Identification of dropouts was possible in the elementary school on the basis of these nine factors. School absence and age of school entrance seemed particularly important in the identification of good readers who may drop out of school prematurely.

Diagnosis of reading disorders in exceptional children

Many exceptional children fail to learn via regular educational procedures. To explore the learning disorders of these children, it is necessary to consider the whole alphabet of key words: aphasia, autism, brain injury, cerebral dysfunction, dyslexia, emotional disturbance, educational retardation, fine motor involvement, gross motor involvement, hyperkinesis, interjacent language disorder, minimal brain pathology, neurological handicap, organic involvement, perceptual impairment, reading disability, Strauss syndrome, and others (Bateman, 1966).

The diagnostic information sought is exact knowledge of how each child learns and of the precise features of the learning environment, such as the teacher's verbal behavior, nature of the reinforcements, and other conditions that are influencing his learning. A combination of developmental history, observation in natural situations of time, multi-factor and single-factor predictive tests, and neurological examinations have been used.

A developmental history is especially important with exceptional children. Although parents' impressions have not been found to be highly reliable, they can be made more accurate and precise by asking simple and specific questions such as: Which of the following phrases describe your child's talking ability at three years, at six, and at the present time?

Not talking at all
Using single words with people who can understand them
Using single words which anyone can understand
Using a few phrases with family
Using a few phrases with other people
Talking in sentences which anyone can understand

Various combinations of tests mentioned in previous chapters have been used in diagnosing the reading achievement of exceptional children. For example, Flower, Viehweg, and Ruzieka (1966) used the following tests:

Vocabulary. Ammons and Ammons Quick Test. No verbal response is required; the children select one of four pictures.
   Vocabulary sub-test of the WISC which gives information on both receptive and expressive vocabulary knowledge.

Verbal reasoning. Abstract Reasoning sub-test of the Differential Aptitude Test by Bennet and others.

Verbal learning. Non-language Multi-mental Test by Terman, McCall, and Lorge.
   A measure of *non-verbal conceptual learning.* Information sub-test of the WISC to measure academic verbal learning.

Comprehension sub-test of the WISC to measure verbal learning in the area of social competency.

Reading. Two sub-tests of the Durrell Analysis of Reading Disability—Oral Reading and Silent Reading.

Using these tests, Flower and his associates found "no consistent differences in language functions peculiar to a group of Kernicteric athetoid children" (1966, p. 67). But, with more normal children auditory deficits seemed to be the factor most closely related to language deficits.

A comparison of the results of the Wide Range Achievement Test (WRAT) and the Gray Oral Reading Paragraphs administered to thirty mentally retarded adults showed marked similarity between the total scores: the Pearson coefficient was .94 ($p < .01$). From the standpoint of merely indicating the individual's reading level, the WRAT seems to be superior (Lawson & Avils, 1962). But it does not yield the diagnostic information about the subject's reading that the Gray test does. Similar studies should be made with a larger number of subjects of different ages and abilities.

It is important to know whether a child's failure to read is due to failure in intake, integration, retention, or output. Actually, the classroom teacher needs special competencies because it is his responsibility continuously to diagnose, guide, and motivate individuals and groups in their learning activities. He needs a diagnostic system that provides insight for instruction based on learning processes. Since each child is unique, the individual case study is the preferred approach to diagnosis.

THE MENTALLY RETARDED

Mentally retarded children, usually described as those scoring between 50 and 70 I.Q., can learn to read well enough to handle life situations. However, total I.Q.'s may be misleading. If a child has a mental age of four on certain sub-tests such as memory, and a mental age of twelve on other sub-tests such as reasoning ability, the child may have a total mental age of only eight. Another child who has a total mental age of eight may have reasoning ability and memory similar to children of four years of age, but otherwise functions like a twelve-year-old. The total I.Q. does not give the clues necessary for the instruction of these children. What is really needed is an analysis of the factors that correlate with slow-learning ability so that remedial instruction can be organized, not only to correct errors in reading, but also to develop more efficient learning in reading and other school subjects (Kirk, 1962, p. 63).

Mentally retarded children may be differentiated from immature children by their lack of ability to accelerate their learning. In many cases, reading disability is a functional, not a structural deficiency; it may not be due to limited potential.

Deficiencies commonly found in the mentally retarded and in other groups of children with learning problems are:

Poor performance on WISC sub-tests of Information, Coding, Arithmetic, and Digit Span, but relatively high on Picture Arrangement and Block Design.

Poor auditory memory and other memory disorders; unless the child is fully occupied with the task at hand and emotionally involved in it.

Inadequate concept formation.

Poor sound-blending ability.

Problems in right-left discrimination of parts of their bodies; e.g., disturbance in bodily orientation.

Inferior intersensory integration, e.g., matching visual with auditory patterns—visual dot patterns with auditory rhythmic taps in the same pattern (auditory-visual equivalence).

Deviant motor patterns.

Inability to write until after they have learned to read.

Spelling disability.

Inability to call up auditory or visual images.

Neurological disturbances.

The mentally retarded tend to score lower on a verbally loaded test than on non-verbal tests or those involving spacial or perceptual factors.

The above characteristics are psycho-motor correlates and/or consequences of reading disability. These, Cawley (1966) believes, should be developed as well as the vocabulary and comprehension abilities measured by most reading tests. There are an indefinite number of adolescents of limited intelligence who are capable of or actually reading on a level of achievement comparable to those with higher intelligence ratings. They may not be working on a higher level because of factors other than that of intelligence. Their mental ages, therefore, should be considered only as an indicator, not as a limit of learning potential. Exceptional children vary so widely in their achievement on different tests that it is practically impossible to describe a mentally retarded child.

Diagnosis should, therefore, be differential; it should give information about the individual's specific abilities.

In diagnosing the reading of mentally retarded children, a major emphasis should be on estimating the child's educability. Mental age, as measured by intelligence tests, does not inalterably indicate a child's capacity to learn. Assessment of his learning capacity is necessary in order to avoid confronting him with too great difficulty or, on the other hand, neglecting to give him the instruction in reading he needs. To assess his ability, it is necessary to take into account his total development and achievement as well as his intellectual status. The time he requires to achieve a specific amount of gain and the quality and accuracy of his response to the learning opportunities provided are other factors that should be considered. To these evidences of educability should be added observation of how the child approaches a reading task, the extent to which he takes initiative, and the satisfaction he experiences (Weiner, 1967).

With mentally retarded children, it is especially important not only to describe the duration and continuity of reading performance but also the setting in which it occurs. Any deviation from an individual's optimum reading development may be traced to the learning environment as well as to factors within the child.

The relevance of a given factor in diagnosing a reading difficulty is indicated if it distinguishes the retarded reader from the normal population, if it correlates with the severity of the retardation, and if it relates to the individual's ability to improve with treatment.

The teacher or clinician uses somewhat different approaches depending upon the causes of the mental retardation.

Any one or a combination of the following conditions may cause or contribute to mental retardation: *1*] neurological deficits, *2*] developmental irregularities, *3*] arrested development, *4*] extreme deprivation of intellectual stimuli, and *5*] emotional disorders.

It is generally agreed that mentally retarded children have potential reading ability that can be developed. Remedial measures should be based on their mental capacities rather than on their weaknesses (Moran, 1960). The instruction should be vital, personal, and practical. It should not be begun until the individual shows or can develop readiness to profit by it, this may not be until a chronological age of ten to twelve. They should have reading materials in line with their interests and everyday experiences, such as road signs and directions of various kinds. The older students are interested in newspapers, want ads, application blanks, descriptions of jobs, and reading required in different kinds of jobs—in short, what they can learn and use now and later.

It may be that the abilities underlying reading achievement can be improved by instruction and practice. Motor coordination can be developed by imaginative physical education activities—walking on a line, balancing, throwing, and catching balls. Finer coordination is acquired in cutting out pictures, copying geometric or other forms. Seeing relationships and telling about events in sequence are developed by recounting a trip they have taken. In fact, many of the usual readiness exercises given by kindergarten and first-grade teachers contribute to pre-reading experiences.

The recognition and remediation of reading disability in the mentally retarded has been neglected. If the overall treatment—oriented objectives for this group—are to be achieved, attention must be paid to their improvement in reading. When given remedial assistance individually or in groups, they improve measurably. Individual treatment for the correction of reading disability can have a therapeutic effect: it helps to prevent social inadequacy and improve mental health and emotional stability; it satisfies some basic needs of these individuals.

The group studied by Daly and Lee (1960) had chronological ages ranging from 10-2 to 18-6, mental ages from 6-1 to 12-7, and I.Q.'s from 45 to 86 with a median of 61. Their expected or potential reading level was estimated from the WISC scores. If a twelve-year-old had a mental age of eight, he might be expected to learn to read at the third-grade level This, of course, is only an approximation, and his progress would be constantly observed with reference to the instruction given. In this experiment, reading disabilities were reported for 38 per cent of the total number examined, and for 48 per cent of the boys. In this situation a poorly designed remedial program without the assistance of a reading specialist showed no significant increase in the aspect stressed, which was reading speed—an inappropriate goal for these individuals.

The less severe mental retardation can be dealt with successfully in the ordinary class. As the degree of backwardness increases, there are children who need to be taught in special classes in special ways. P. E. Vernon (1956) stated that apparently dull children are not inevitably backward, even though they have a low I.Q., the teacher should do his best to explore the underlying causes. It is possible that they could learn in a changed environment with medical attention, or with a new approach to teaching.

THE EMOTIONALLY DISTURBED

Emotional disturbances may arise from failure in reading or from some common causation. In an indefinite number of cases, the emotional disturbance prevents the child from concentrating on the reading task; it distracts his attention. However, emotional disturbances do not necessarily interfere with achievement in reading. Although reading difficulties and emotional disturbances occur in the same children, less than 3 per cent of the 500 girls and about 25 per cent of the boys at the Hawthorne Center for disturbed children of normal intelligence showed primary reading disability. From 60 to 65 per cent of this total group was achieving adequately on the California

Achievement Test (Rabinovitch, 1964). However, certain other groups, Rabinovitch pointed out, do contain large numbers of children who have primary reading disabilities. According to a survey carried on at another psychiatric clinic (Roman, 1957), as many as 84 per cent of the problems of personality disorders and anti-social behavior were found to be associated with reading problems.

An auditory and kinesthetic approach was used for one class period a day over a period of three months with a group of 24 emotionally disturbed children two years or more retarded in reading (Talmadge, Davids & Laufer, 1963). Of these, 14 showed indications of cortical dysfunction or impairment; 10 gave no indication of neurological dysfunction. The children engaged in activities such as the following: *1*] recognition of likenesses and differences in configuration patterns, using objects and letter forms;   *2*] classification of objects according to initial sound;   *3*] recognition of different vowel sounds by circling all the *a's* in a selection.

In addition to the perceptual-motor program, emotionally disturbed children need a socialization program. At the Dubnoff School for Educational Therapy, severely disturbed children first learn to establish a satisfactory one-to-one relationship with a trained adult. As the child begins to respond to the demands of the teacher and of reality, he is placed in a small group. In this socialization process, the teacher first takes an active part in providing a progression of activities that the child can handle at his present stage of emotional control. He learns to share tools and equipment, to wait his turn, and to take an interest in his classmates' activities. The morning greeting may be extended to a sharing of experiences and later to the writing of a group newspaper or diary record. The physical aspects of the classroom setting, such as the placement of chairs for optimum communication, contribute both to socialization and to perceptual-motor training. As the children become more aware of one another, their behavior is increasingly influenced by peer approval or disapproval. The small group classroom activities are extended by the structured playground activities, thus paving the way for transition to regular classrooms (Dubnoff, 1966, pp. 7-9).

Reading problems associated with emotional disturbances are difficult to treat. At Rockland State Psychiatric Hospital the staff used many approaches to the teaching of reading but with little success. The repeated failure of some children to learn caused their increased resistance to classroom situations (Barclay, 1966). The regular staff of teachers, experienced in teaching emotionally disturbed children, introduced the Initial Teaching Alphabet (i.t.a.) after a three-day training workshop. In a unit of 150 boys six to twelve years old, 75 were selected for participation in the study. They were divided into three groups of matched pairs according to age and I.Q. The mean chronological age was nine; the mean mental age, seven; and the I.Q., 79. Groups I and II were schizophrenic cases; Groups III and IV primary behavior problems; and V and VI, psychotic cases. As measured by the California Achievement Test, those taught with i.t.a. progressed about thirty per cent more rapidly than those taught with traditional orthography. They did not experience difficulty in making the transition from i.t.a. to traditional orthography. A change from passive-defensive, withdrawn, or uncooperative behavior to better attitudes was also noted.

A similar experiment carried out by Barclay (1966) with eight older boys, ten to fourteen years, who were non-readers and had not profited by four years of instruction, obtained similar results. They progressed almost three times as rapidly as children in the traditional group. In the i.t.a. groups there were no serious behavior problems, practically no truancy, a happy atmosphere, and a sense of shared achievement. Thus it was not necessary to waste time trying to sidetrack destructive activities. The more rapid development of reading skills was made by the older pupils. They did not lose in reading skills during the summer. Much of the work was on a tutorial or individual basis because group reading could not always be initiated. All the teachers wanted to continue the i.t.a. program.

Another method was used with eight neurologically impaired, mentally retarded, and severely emotionally disturbed children at the Neuropsychiatric Institute School, University of California, Los Angeles. This experimental reading program (Hewett, Mayhew, & Rabb, 1967) featured: *1*] small increments of learning, gradually increasing in difficulty; *2*] immediate rewards for correct responses in the form of praise and extrinsic motivation; *3*] withholding of praise for incorrect responses; *4*] systematic word reviews, discrimination exercises, and comprehension questions; *5*] supplementary reading of books; and *6*] detailed records kept of the responses and needs of each child. All eight children made some progress. Since even children with limited ability need success in reading to build up their self-concept, it was felt that:

> . . . establishment of rigid criteria for inclusion or rejection of children with respect to reading instruction is highly undesirable and that every child should be given an opportunity to acquire some level of proficiency with this vital skill. (Hewett, *et al.,* 1967, p. 47)

The structured lesson and reinforcement of success were thought to be most responsible for the success of the programed approach; progress became a motivating factor.

Still more determined was the intensive effort to teach learning skills to disturbed delinquent boys ten to twelve years of age (Minuehin, Chamberlain, & Graubard, 1967). The main and unique features of this program were the children's dual roles of participant and observer and the explicit goals for each session. As participants, they interacted with others in the class; as observers, they watched their peers through a one-way-vision screen and rated their behavior. In rating others, they learned to evaluate behavior, and, being aware that they in turn were being observed, they observed their own behavior more critically. The language arts lessons focused on listening, taking turns and sharing in communication, telling a simple story, asking related cogent questions. These skills were taught largely through games, role playing, and group discussion. Important factors in their learning were specific goals, small learning steps, mastery and success, self- and peer-evaluation based on objective criteria.

The results were a marked increase in attention, ability to

appraise behavior, increased relevant verbal responses, and facility in using communication rules to facilitate gathering and ordering information.

In his experiment on the education of emotionally disturbed children, Hobbs (1966, p. 1111) emphasized the importance of developing competence in these children: "Special therapy rooms are not needed; the classroom is a natural setting for a constructive relationship between a disturbed child and a competent, concerned adult." The use of stories that present problems similar to those which a disturbed child is facing and portrays characters with whom he can identify has been suggested as helpful with emotionally disturbed children. But this technique must be handled skillfully by a trained person. Livengood (1961) found that sixth-grade children low in intelligence and social acceptance seemed to gain socially from having thirty-six literary selections read to them. The group as a whole, however, while showing gains in personality traits, seemed to lose in good relations and democratic practices.

THE BILINGUAL AND THE DISADVANTAGED

With speakers of other languages and dialects the language problems—listening, speaking, reading, and writing—are severe. Many articles and books have recently been published about this problem (Whipple & Black, 1966). The following seem to be sound basic procedures:

1] Accept and appreciate their present language and the best in their culture, while pointing out the advantages of their becoming competent in the use of standard English.

2] Give much practice in sentence structure and the sounds of English through interesting natural conversations and dialogues, some of them based on the content of other subjects.

3] After the student has learned to pronounce a word, phrase, sentence, or paragraph with accurate articulation and natural intonation and stress, have him write it and read it.

4]   Teach basic sight vocabulary through sentences, and word recognition skills through systematic application of context clues, phonics, structural analysis, and use of the dictionary as they meet unfamiliar words when reading something they enjoy or need to know about.

5]   Provide additional instruction for those who are having special difficulties in pronunciation, with English idioms, or other difficulties.

6]   Provide wide reading of interesting material on their present silent-reading level.

7]   Make reading rewarding—enjoyable, worth while, practical, successful.

THE GIFTED

The diagnosis of gifted children's reading achievement has generally been neglected. Their scores on standardized and informal tests and average marks on their report cards often conceal their failure to reach their reading potential. Although some gifted children have developed efficient reading methods of their own, many have not learned to vary their rate and method of reading with the kind of materials or to read a long chapter, article, or poem adequately. They have not acquired the techniques of deeper interpretive, critical, or creative reading.

The principles and procedures of diagnosis and remediation suggested for these groups can be applied in modified form to other groups. The essence of diagnosis is sensitivity to the individual's expectations, his feelings about himself and his reading, his responses to the instruction given, and the interaction of all the factors involved in his reading achievement.

6. Remediation of reading disabilities

Remediation receives almost no attention. There is no treatment of remedial procedures comparable to the comprehensive overviews of reading problems by Malmquist (1960), Flower, Gofman, and Lawson (1965), and Russell and Fea (1963). There has been much more research on diagnosis than on remediation. Yet, if any ability is worth testing, it is worth teaching.

Most specific information on remediation has been obtained from case studies. Many other studies have reported progress in reading resulting from group instruction. When there is little difference between the results of individual and group instruction, the small groups are preferable from the standpoint of economy of teacher time and possible beneficial interaction among members of the group (Lovell, Johnson, & Platts, 1962). Unfortunately, many of the reports on remedial programs give the results of the program but do not describe the specific methods and materials by which those results were obtained.

A number of remedial methods have been suggested, some specific for a certain reading ability, others more generally applicable; a very few are substantiated by research, others grow out of experience.

Much of the research has been devoted to perceptual training and the treatment of severe reading disability often attributed to neurological deficits or dysfunction. Many reports of remedial reading programs have been published but constitute another area for review in a separate monograph. Still less attention has been given to determining the effectiveness of preventive or developmental programs.

Pilot studies such as those by Cruickshank, Bentzen, Ratzeburg, and Tannhauser (1961), which try out classroom procedures derived from theory and principles, give teachers suggestions for methods of working with brain-injured and hyperactive children. By observing the responses of their pupils to the procedures and materials that they use, teachers can judge the effectiveness of the methods and materials for certain individuals. The methods and materials described in Cruickshank's 125-page chapter are based on four main principles which would be applicable to most remedial work with severely retarded readers:

> . . . *a*) the reduction of unessential visual and auditory stimuli; *b*) the reduction of environmental space; *c*) the establishment of a highly structured program; and *d*) the increase of the stimulus value of the instruction materials themselves. (Bateman, 1966, p. 111)

Although a control group was set up, it was not, as Cruickshank and his colleagues themselves emphasized, possible to control all the variables that might influence the subjects' achievement. The majority of the children in both experimental and control groups made progress in reading and other academic subjects. The experimental groups made a few statistically significant greater gains than the control group during the first year; these gains were not maintained in the second year, and only three of the original 45 children were ever placed in regular classes. It is very difficult for this type of severely handicapped child to achieve normal language facility or vocational goals. Although brain-injured retarded children show improvement during the period of tutoring, they tend to regress when the special stimulation is discontinued (Gallagher, 1962b). These children seem to need continued remedial support.

In working with reading problems, the teacher or clinician needs not only an understanding of possible correlates and causative factors, but also a repertory of remedial techniques on which he can draw, selecting the ones that seem more appropriate to the particular case. Research studies give some indication of procedures that have proved most effective with other individuals and groups.

Remediation is usually approached through specific exercises to improve specific skills, e.g. practice in recognition of the

Dolch basic sight vocabulary, exercises in visual and auditory discrimination, and the like.

However, there is quite a different way of viewing remediation: first, by analyzing the learning process involved in each reading task; and, second, by arranging an environment to facilitate learning. A favorable environment is one in which the teacher guides rather than tells, understands rather than acquiesces, and provides experiences rather than using a laissez-faire approach. In such an environment, the students feel important as individuals. They are aware of the methods that bring success. The teacher gives genuine praise for the child's real and appropriate progress, unobtrusive help when progress is blocked.

Running through many research findings on all educational levels and in different aspects of reading is the importance of meaningful materials for developing comprehension, speed, and retention.

If an individual has the tendency to interject his own personal experiences into his reading, he is more likely to fail to comprehend the author's thought. Two kinds of material are likely to reflect this tendency in a response pattern: first, material written in the first person; and, second, material with a strong affective content which evokes personal association (Cromer & Wiener, 1966). With content of these kinds, the individual starts reading but soon begins to follow his own train of thought. He is likely to make fewer errors when reading about high-and-far-off times than about the here-and-now. Poor readers are more likely to make idiosyncratic responses than good readers. The number of reading errors tend to be increased by any condition that increases the likelihood of self-reference.

Experience reading, if carried too far, may over-encourage the use of personal reference and prevent the child from becoming familiar with the sequences common to different kinds of reading material. Reading involves some kind of sequential or syntactic relationship among the individual words.

Various automated instructional procedures have been used with retarded readers to help them acquire word recognition, spelling, and reading skills. These methods have proved to be more effective than some classroom instruction, but not more effective than individual tutoring.

Programed material is more appropriate for learning skills than for complicated thought processes. Being teacher controlled, it offers little or no opportunity for pupil initiative and creativity. Some individuals are stimulated by programed material; others need a social stimulus. Boys tend to respond better than girls.

Results of remedial instruction

Remedial instruction should result in improvement both in reading ability and in attitudes toward reading and toward oneself. The latter is the more pervasive. If attitudes are modified, progress is likely to continue after the special instruction is discontinued. One of the few studies that attempted to measure attitudes obtained evidence that "remedial education, as organized in this investigation, was on the whole effective in improving the reading ability of severely retarded nine-year-old children of about average intelligence" (Dunham, 1960, p. 175). The effect on the reading achievement of the twenty children was greater than the effect on their attitudes as measured by a modification of the Thurstone attitude scale. An examination of individual children's records showed that some children in the group made little progress and some even lost ground.

Gains resulting from remedial instruction have often been exaggerated. Instead of a simple test-retest procedure. Curr and Gourlay (1960) determined the "true" gain as the amount by which the gross gain of the remedial group exceeded the gross gain of the controls. Although the gross gains of the remedial group were comparable with gains reported for other investigations, appreciable gains were also made by the controls. Consequently the "true" gains were small, although a statistically significant "true" gain was obtained on the Schonell Reading Comprehension Test. Data also showed "the impermanence of the net gains made by the pupils receiving remedial education" (Curr & Gourlay, 1960, p. 155).

Modes of learning

Patterns of modality should be recognized. Any inherent preference for one modality such as visual versus auditory or part versus whole should be capitalized in order that the individual experience as much success as possible. At the same time, training in the individual's greatest perceptual, cognitive, or linguistic deficit should be given to the extent to which such training is profitable.

WHOLE OR PART MODALITIES

Although global reading is characteristic of good readers, it may not be possible for beginners to turn an undifferentiated whole into its constituent elements. Actually, analysis of wholes and integration of parts occur simultaneously in good reading (de Hirsch, 1963, p. 381). The reader recognizes words both by their configurations and by their sequence of letters and determining features. But some individuals, especially the good readers, tend to focus on wholes; other, more often the poor readers, on parts (Helen M. Robinson, 1964).

VISUAL OR AUDITORY MODALITIES

To grasp the meaning of an unfamiliar word, unskilled or beginning readers need to say it or form the spoken word with their lips. Even fluent readers may evoke auditory and motor images of which they are scarcely aware and may resort to obvious vocalization when they meet an unfamiliar word. The highly skilled reader may make a direct association between significant clues in the printed symbol and its meaning.

Kindergarten children learned similar words faster when they were accompanied by a picture or when they said the word instead of just hearing it. With dissimilar words, the kind of clue made little difference; hearing the word was even slightly more effective (King & Muehl, 1965).

To obtain information on the preferred sensory mode of fifty-six average and retarded second-grade readers, Budoff and Quinlan (1964) presented meaningful words both orally and visually. The visual task was to recognize the word exposed for .5 of a second. The aural task was to identify pairs of words presented orally on a magnetic tape with loudness held constant. Word pairs such as *want, play; spot, cow* were used. Only nouns and verbs were included. The pairs were presented visually first to half of the children and orally first to the other half. In general, the auditory presentations resulted in more rapid rate of learning with   *1*] primary grade children,   *2*] poor readers, and   *3*] low-ability children. The discrepancy between the two modalities was more extreme for the retarded readers. In the second grade, retarded readers, in general, learned better by auditory than by visual presentation.

In grades four, five, and six, and in high school, retarded readers tended to be relatively better aural and relatively poorer visual learners than the average readers. The average readers also showed less discrepancy in rate of learning by the two modes of presentation. Unselected college students favored the visual mode of presentation. The superior readers learned better with the visual presentation. The visual approach also seemed better with difficult material.

Stuart (1967), using the short form of the Witkin Embedded Figure Test as a measure of perceptual style, found successful readers in the seventh and eighth grades less dependent on the preceptual field. The relationship between reading grade level and verbal I.Q. was much stronger.

These relationships may not hold for bilingual and Negro disadvantaged children who speak another language or dialect. Their habitual speech, spelling patterns, and sentence structure, being different from the standard pronunciation of the printed

words, may make decoding of the printed symbols confusing to
them.

When drawings of common objects were used to teach the
meaning of words, Katz and Deutsch (1964) found this form of
visual presentation to be superior with retarded readers. A combined auditory and picture presentation was next best; the auditory presentation was least effective. The speed at which the
materials are presented may also make a difference in the favored mode of learning. The visual presentation usually became
more efficient than the audio at around 300 words per minute.
The audio-visual was superior to the other modes at different
speeds.

The ability to transfer from one modality to another is related to intelligence at grades one, two, and three. For these
grades, Birch and Belmont (1965) obtained correlations of .56,
.42, and .57. At grade four, the correlations began to decline
and continued to become lower through grade six—.41, .34, .28,
respectively. Correlations between the Auditory-Visual Pattern
Test and reading achievement declined from grade one (.70) to
grade two (.42) and continued to decline through grade five
(.41, .34, .28). In contrast, the correlation between I.Q. and
reading increased from .27 at grade four to .69 at grade five and
.83 at grade six (Birch & Belmont, 1965).

The teacher or clinician should be alert to the preferred
modality of individual children and capitalize on their most
efficient ways of learning. Poor readers who are good aural
learners and who have high listening comprehension should be
able to profit a great deal from remedial work that features
aural learning skills. At the same time, they may be given practice in visual perception, discrimination, and memory, and in
using a combination of modalities in their reading.

In beginning reading, a combination of two sensory channels—auditory and visual—was more efficient with less able
learners than a single sensory channel. Writing the words being
taught further aided retention for some subjects.

Visual and perceptual training

Visual training helps the individual to use his eyes more efficiently. Inefficient use of the eyes in reading, much more than visual acuity, is involved—fusional amplitude; fixation, convergence, and accommodation abilities; and speed and span of perception. These abilities may be improved by orthoptics—ocular re-education (Anapolle, 1967).

It is also useful to know the clues to word recall used by non-readers and beginning readers in kindergarten and grade one. Marchbanks and Levin (1965) systematically examined four clues: *1*] shape of the word, *2*] first letter and third letter of three-letter words, *3*] shape, and *4*] the five letters of five-letter words. The first letter of both long and short word forms was the clue most frequently used by both kindergarten children and children who has had approximately five months of reading instruction. Last letters were used second in frequency, except for first-grade girls. Kindergarten boys' use of last as well as first letters may be associated with boys' greater tendency to reversals. The clue least used was shape.

Visual perception, as stated in chapter two, correlates with reading. A definite relationship has been shown between difficulties in visual perception and lack of achievement in reading. However, perceptual abilities appear to be more important in the beginning stages of reading. The maximum of perceptual development in normal children usually occurs between the ages of four and seven. Around the second grade, the process of concept realization gradually takes over.

Can reading achievement be altered by perceptual training? Is skill in perception linked with reading achievement? These are questions of practical concern to teachers and clinicians. There is not much use in making a diagnosis unless the deficits discovered can be overcome. Evidence of the effectiveness of perceptual training, like so many other areas of reading research, is conflicting, perhaps partly due to differences in effectiveness of the various training methods used as well as to other factors already mentioned as influencing research results.

Tachistoscopic training which uses the Gestalt or whole-word approach is reported to be effective with children who have basic vocabulary skills, but not with first-grade children (Goins, 1958). The effectiveness of tachistoscopic training may also be greater with whole perceivers. Goins found that children with low scores on the picture-squares test approached each item individually, whereas those with high scores perceived the group of pictures as a unit.

The Frostig Program for the Development of Visual Perception (Frostig & Harne, 1964) gives training in some abilities measured in Frostig's test of visual perception.

Other kinds of perceptual training have been given with varying degrees of success. Rutherford (1964) found a perceptual-motor training program effective with kindergarten children in promoting readiness measured by the Metropolitan Reading-Readiness Test. Hagin, Silver, and Hersh (1965) reported an apparently highly successful activity program. The subjects were twenty boys with reading disabilities, ranging in age from eight to eleven years, with WISC I.Q.'s above 85. They were paired on age, I.Q., and initial perceptual deficits. Every child was scheduled for two 45-minute individual sessions per week for six months. One member of the pair received perceptual training in areas of his maximal deficit, e.g. spacial orientation or sound discrimination; while the other received basal reading instruction from the same teacher. The common denominator underlying all the perceptual problems appeared to be difficulty in spatial and temporal organization. Training was given at three levels: the "accuracy level" to improve a given perceptual ability; the "inter-modal level" to improve the integration of one modality with another; and the "verbal level to relate to perception of oral and written language" (Hagin, Silver, & Hersh, 1965, p. 368). For example, the accurate perception of forms ranging from simple forms to complex forms were first taught through a three-step process: visual matching, copying, and recall. Each step in the sequence was to be mastered before the next step was introduced. If the child had difficulty, he was given additional clues which were reduced as he showed proficiency.

Each subject served as his own control in the comparison of initial and re-test scores. Only direction of change, not magnitude, was reported.

The group which received perceptual training made significant improvement on the Bender-Gestalt, the Marble Board Test, a tactile figure-background test, the Extension Test showing conflict between the arm elevated and the preferred hand, and a right-left discrimination test. They also improved in measures of reading: the Wide Range Achievement Test, both Reading and Spelling sections; and the Metropolitan Reading Achievement Test. The comparison group that received individual conventional reading instruction did not make significant improvement in any of these tests. Possible explanations of the lack of improvement of the comparison group are that the basal-reader instruction was not appropriate to these children with special reading disabilities or the instruction was not as expert or as enthusiastically given as it might have been. The authors suggested that "perceptual training stimulates neurological maturation to a level appropriate for reading" (Hagin, Silver, & Hersh, 1965, p. 370).

Another experiment in perceptual training (Chansky, 1963a) obtained less favorable results, although both perceptual training and perceptual task orientation showed promise. Chansky gave practice to third- and fourth-grade underachievers in visual discrimination, left-right orientation, and organization of visual non-verbal stimuli. Of the 34 children, 12 received both reading readiness and perceptual training, 8 received reading readiness but no perceptual training, and 7 received no reading readiness but perceptual training. Reading achievement was measured by the Gilmore Oral Reading Test and spelling by the sub-test of the Metropolitan Achievement Test. All three groups received ten weekly sessions lasting thirty to forty-five minutes. The experimental materials were the Halsam Products Company, Blockville Set # 103, consisting of two main block shapes; triangles and rectangles (see description in article). With these blocks, the children tried to reproduce a design that was suggested each session. After they had completed a design, they were given help in the planning, in orientation, in ability to make inferences, and in ability to make discriminations—the factors on which the children's performance was scored. The designs presented were arranged from the easiest to the most difficult.

The group receiving no reading readiness and no perceptual training "made significantly greater improvement in word accuracy than any other group" (Chansky, 1963a, p. 37). In other words, neither remedial reading nor this kind of perceptual training resulted in improvement in word accuracy. But the children of high intelligence and the initially good readers who were given perceptual training made the greater gains. The results on improvement in reading comprehension were similar with respect to the lack of effect of perceptual training but not with respect to the influence of intelligence. In spelling, however, significantly greater gains were made by the group receiving perceptual training. The control group made no comparable improvement in either reading or spelling.

In perceptual training, it is important to recognize visual perception as a developmental process. The perception of the young child is caught and held by the dominant aspects of the visual field. This may be an explanation of why letters and words in color are effective: they center the child's attention on the letters in color, which are the ones to be learned. As the child grows older, the domination by the field decreases and the role of a higher order of perceptual organization becomes more important. Perception should be recognized as an intermediate process between sensation and thought. A given sensation is associated with meaning and significance. It can then be used as a tool to thinking.

In three experiments, Gibson, Bishop, Schiff, and Smith (1964) found that the perception and retention of verbal material by college students is aided by the meaningfulness and pronunciability of the words presented.

Words are also recognized visually by college students more quickly when they are presented closer together. Recall is easier in context than when words are presented in isolation

(Morton, 1965). No relation was found between recall of words seen and such structural factors as length of word and number of ascenders and descenders. Among the sources of errors analyzed were expectancy, previous stimuli and responses, and inadequate perception.

Training in auditory perception

For the large majority of children, proficiency in visual and auditory perception and the integration of these two modalities are essential to achievement in reading. Deutsch (1964) found highly significant differences between good and poor readers on the Wepman Auditory Discrimination Test in grades one and three; less difference in grade five; but all differences favored good readers. In another sample, Deutsch found significant coefficients of correlation between scores on the Wepman and the WISC comprehension sub-test for both good and poor readers. She concluded that poor readers have greater difficulty in auditory discrimination and in shifting from one modality to another. Deutsch postulated a minimal level of auditory discrimination which, if reached, no longer influences reading achievement.

Individual and classroom activities to strengthen the abilities diagnosed by the ITPA have been described in a number of articles. Among these are activities with the tape recorder, vocabulary games such as "Password," and quick oral questions for training in auditory decoding. Filmstrips, movies, TV programs, and other exercises in observation are used for training in visual decoding. Similar simple classroom activities are suggested for the other psycholinguistic abilities. Everyday activities such as repeating a series of words such as a grocery list, learning one's telephone number, address and zip code number, and filling in the words in incomplete sentences help to develop and strengthen a child's auditor-vocal sequences and automatic-auditory vocal ability.

A few specific remedial techniques

With the exception of Fernald's (1943) kinesthetic method, the visual-kinesthetic method developed by Hegge, Kirk, and Kirk (1955), the phonic exercises of Gillingham and Stillman (1940), and the multi-sensory approaches described in the annual bulletins of The Orton Society, 1951 to 1964, there have been few detailed descriptions of specific remedial techniques.

PROGRESSIVE-CHOICE METHOD

The general principle of reducing the initial complexity of the reading task while providing for a progression of learning experiences is applicable to most cases of reading disability. Davy (1962) described a "progressive-choice method" in some detail. The procedure was to simplify the presentation of stimuli by presenting each letter initially as only one sound at one time and combining each new sound-letter association into meaningful words before teaching another letter sound. For example, *m* and *o* which are easily discriminable would be taught, and the child would read the word *mom* using these two letters. Each additional letter learned, *a, c, t,* enabled the pupils to read many words they had never seen before and also stories built from the letter sounds they had learned. A variety of other activities were also included such as coloring large letters, sounding them out as they worked, playing games, and writing the letters and words they had learned to develop auditory and visual skills. More detail of the progressive-choice method is given in the article (Davy, 1962, p. 276). By using an orderly sequence of easily discriminable items, pupils have learned to read more effectively than by the usual basal-reader method.

THE INITIAL TEACHING ALPHABET (I.T.A.)

i.t.a. has been used successfully with some remedial cases. In beginning reading, confusion resulting from different sounds for the same letter forms and vice versa is avoided by a new alphabet in which there is a one-to-one relationship between the 44 sounds of English and the graphic symbols that represent them.

Two experiments were carried on by Peters (1967) to compare the spelling errors made by children taught by three methods: the look-and-say, the phonic, and the i.t.a. Peters found that the i.t.a. produced the fewest omissions, insertions, and perseverations. The other two methods produced the fewest number of certain other kinds of errors. Overall spelling attainment did not seem to be affected, but perceptual and rule-following skills did influence spelling favorably. Apparently children taught by i.t.a. "have the sort of non-redundant skeletal structure from which conventional English spellings can be readily developed" (Peters, 1967, pp. 52-53).

Another study of the attainments in reading and spelling of children who learned to read through i.t.a. found no difference in reading achievement that could be attributed to either i.t.a. or the use of traditional orthography. Spelling was not adversely affected by i.t.a. Girls were better than boys, whatever the method, though boys seemed to benefit more from i.t.a. than girls (Swales, 1967). These are only two of the many recent experiments on the effect of the i.t.a. on reading and spelling achievement. Although comparisons of i.t.a. with other methods are inconclusive, there is evidence that, in the beginning stage, children learn to read more easily and quickly by the i.t.a., write more freely in the "new alphabet," but the difference in later reading achievement between the i.t.a. and basal reader methods is not statistically significant.

TEACHING CONNECTIVES

Many words in the Dolch list are connectives or function words such as prepositions, adverbs, and conjunctions: *although, however, thus.* Children who stumble over these words need help in the understanding of the words and constructions in which they occur (Robertson, 1966). To help children gain an understanding of these words, the teacher may devise practical activities that illustrate the use of the words. One might say, and demonstrate: "*When* Tommy comes back, Jane may leave the room." "*When* everyone is quiet, I will read the story." Such activities might be accompanied by a discussion of the role these structure words play in the sentences.

WORD ATTACK SKILLS

When a student meets an unfamiliar word, are there any techniques for identifying it that are relatively effective? H.A. Robinson (1963) asked bright fourth-grade children to use a succession of skills beginning with the ones most frequently used and adding more as necessary to achieve word recognition. He found that context clues alone were not sufficient for the identification of unfamiliar words. Noting the configuration of the word did not contribute much more to the identification of the word. Addition of phonic and/or structural elements in initial positions resulted in little more success. Using all these techniques in turn enabled only one-fourth of the sixty-one subjects to identify fifty per cent or more of the words. With this group of children, no word-identification technique was used very successfully. More effective methods of instruction should be developed to teach this basic reading skill.

THE KINESTHETIC METHOD

If a child is a "kinesthetic learner," he may make progress in reading through the Fernald (1943) kinesthetic or tracing method when he has failed to learn by visual-auditory techniques (Ofman & Shaevitz, 1963). An elaboration of the Fernald technique (method A) used by Roberts and Coleman (1958) was definitely superior in teaching retarded readers between the ages of nine and eleven years to two other methods: one stressing cooperative activities; and the other, competition, using a system of awards by stars with prizes at the end of the term. In method A, the child chose a difficult word he wanted to learn. The teacher wrote it on a piece of paper, and the child traced it with his forefinger, pronouncing its component parts as he traced them. He continued this process until he could write the word without looking at it. All the children were invited to use the method for learning a word. The child then chose a topic and wrote his story on one side of his paper. Any word he could not spell the teacher wrote on the back of his paper in fairly large letters. For these words he also used the method of tracing: vocalization-writing. When he had finished the story, the teacher reprinted it and pasted it in the child's own storybook. He read the story to the teacher. Often the children would read their stories to their classmates or read silently each others' stories. This process encouraged curiosity and creativity, it was concerned with the child's interest; and it increased self-confidence through writing, reading, and exhibiting their work. Also, it involved the child. Motivation was from within, not superimposed by the teacher. As their storybook grew, they got a sense of accomplishment, of progress. For recreational reading, they could choose their own books. By combining reading, speaking, and writing, they attained proficiency in all three.

USE OF COLOR

With young children, 3.5 to 5.1 years of age, who had not yet been taught to recognize either words or letters, the task of matching black letters and words was at least three times as difficult as the same task when letters were printed, each in a distinctive color (Jones, 1965).

WORKBOOKS

How effective are reading workbooks? The answer, of course, would vary with the workbook used and the method of using it. The Scott Foresman reading-readiness workbook, *We Read Pictures,* used with first-grade children for a nine-week period at the end of the year, was less effective in developing visual discrimination as measured by the Murphy-Durrell diagnostic reading-readiness test than was an informal program using no commercially prepared material (Weeks, 1964). Nor did the workbook program increase auditory discrimination and learning rate. Chronological age and maturity were associated with readiness as tested. The method of giving retarded readers extra practice in workbooks should be subjected to detailed observation of the learning that actually results from the experience.

AUDIO-VISUAL AIDS

For individuals diagnosed as having reading problems due to their foreign-language background, audio-visual material has been used successfully. Since Spanish-speaking pupils have special difficulties in comprehending the abstractions expressed in the English language, Cline (1965) used, with an experimental group of 151 children in the fourth grade for one-half hour each day, films, filmstrips, records, slides, pictures, and other audiovisual materials which correlated closely with their textbooks. Progress was measured by the California Achievement Tests and the Gilmore Oral Reading Test. The subjects read the Gilmore oral paragraphs, and their voices were evaluated by members of the speech department. Over the entire period of the project the experimental group achieved 100 per cent of their expected gain; the control group, 76 per cent, a statistically significant difference.

MACHINE-CENTERED METHODS

Over the years there have been many research studies on eye movements in reading (Tinker, 1958; Gilbert, 1959) which have compared a material-centered approach with a machine-centered approach. Long's (1962) experiment is fairly typical. Undergraduates spent eight weeks in reading-improvement

classes: half used only printed material in an instructional program; the other half used only mechanical devices—the tachistoscope and the controlled reader. Both groups improved. The
printed materials and the mechanical devices seemed to be
equally effective in producing gains in reading rate and level of
comprehension, although the printed material proved more effective for improving paragraph comprehension. The main
questions raised in considering the use of mechanical devices
are:

> Can they be adjusted to individual differences?
>
> Do habits of reading while using the machine transfer to
> the reading of books?
>
> Do the gains in rate persist after the training is
> discontinued?
>
> Might the mechanical pressures disrupt the efficient
> habits that certain good readers have acquired?
>
> Might the emphasis on speech and no regressive
> movements prevent deliberative reading and deeper
> interpretation?
>
> Can improvement in rate of comprehension for different
> purposes be achieved more effectively by instruction
> in other than that which is machine-centered?

"ADVANCED ORGANIZERS"

On a higher level of comprehension an introduction, or
"advanced organizer," may aid remedial cases in comprehending and remembering unfamiliar material. One purpose of the
"organizer" is to clarify and make more discriminable the new
concepts and to supply a framework or structure with reference
to the reader's previously acquired ideas. Such an introduction
should delineate clearly and precisely the main similarities and
differences between the new ideas in the selection and the reader's previous ideas or cognitive structure. If this is done, the
new ideas should be comprehended more easily and accurately
and should be remembered because they are connected with a
pattern of thought already in the reader's mind. Ausubel and
Fitzgerald (1961) tested the effect of such introductory ma-

terial on the learning and retention of the new ideas by 155 undergraduate seniors. They reported significantly higher scores on the retention of the new material for the students who had been given the introductory material. This technique might well be used with remedial cases who have difficulty in remembering what they read.

DRUGS

The use of drugs in the treatment of learning disabilities has barely been explored. Certain drugs can sometimes make children more receptive to learning by indirectly increasing attention span and decreasing distractibility. The use of a drug, Deanol, as an energizer to increase the effectiveness of instruction with children who did not respond to the usual remedial methods has been studied by six investigators, all of whom reported increases in speed and efficiency of reading and facility in perception as a result of medication (Harvey, 1966). However, two investigators (Staiger, 1961; Valusek, 1963) found no favorable effect on reading as a result of its use. Although the drug increased perceptual speed as measured by clerical speed and accuracy, it did not influence the more complex intellectual activity of reading to any great extent. The side effects of any drug and its temporary effect on learning must be considered in any investigation of this kind.

HYPNOTISM

Hypnotism has also been suggested as a method of treating severe reading problems. The soundest point of view with respect to this possibility is to exercise great caution. Hypnosis does not cure any difficulty but may make a person more accessible to treatment. However, there is the great danger that it may release undesirable tendencies as well as remove detrimental blocks.

COUNSELING

Counseling combined with reading instruction was found to be effective with two small groups, one elementary and one secondary (Strickler, 1964). Both groups showed gains in reading performance and in more positive school and social attitudes. The elementary group benefited more from the remedial treatment than did the secondary retarded readers.

Although the need for counseling is indicated by the diagnosis of many reading problems, it is difficult to obtain statistical evidence of the effectiveness of counseling on groups. Winkler, Teigland, Munger, and Kranzler (1965) studied the effects of counseling on 700 under-achieving fourth graders. They did not obtain evidence of significant change either in grade-point average or measured personality variables. To improve achievement, instruction in the specific reading difficulties as well as modification of underlying personality factors is necessary. A global approach aimed at both increasing ego strength and developing specific reading skills should be most effective.

INVOLVEMENT OF TEACHERS AND PARENTS

Involvement of teachers and parents is important in most remedial reading cases. Since a child's reading development and difficulties depend a great deal upon conditions adults have provided for his learning, teachers and parents should both be involved in the remedial program. Peck, Zwerling, Rabban, and Mendelsohn (1966) held small group discussions with teachers to help them understand their own feelings about the school situations and to enhance their awareness and understanding of emotional and clinical factors related to the child's success and failure in reading. The aim was to help them develop a more favorable attitude toward the child and perceive him in a new light.

Similar small group discussions with the parents likewise helped them to express their feelings about school and teachers and increased their "awareness of parental practices, attitudes, and family atmosphere as factors in the child's total functioning" (Peck, *et al.*, 1966, p. 432). Ryan (1964) found that a planned program of parental participation was more effective than incidental participation as shown by second-grade children's progress. The experimental group was superior to the control group on the word-meaning test; they read more extensively, visted the library more frequently, and expected less help with new words from parents. They were not superior to the control group on paragraph meaning, a skill which parents would not be expected to teach.

Other key school personnel should also be involved if the school atmosphere and curriculum is to be improved. This is the "systems approach" which interrelates all aspects of home, school, and community related to the individual.

Examples of remedial programs

There are three general essentials for successful remedial work: a curriculum designed to meet individual needs, appropriate teaching techniques, and the child's responsiveness to the learning situation. The situation should also provide progression of experiences which result in behavioral modification which the students themselves can recognize. They engage in more creative activities. They make appropriate responses to the situation and internalize control and direction within themselves. The test is whether they are able, after a period of special instruction in reading, to return to their regular class.

At the Dubnoff School for Educational Therapy in North Hollywood, California, two aspects are considered most basic to learning and rehabilitation: "ego integration dealing with body schema and body image; and visual-perceptual-motor development" (Dubnoff, 1966, p. 3). Diagnostic procedures are necessary to detect such deficiencies. Any deficiency in one area of perception, such as in tactile perception, may cause difficulty in other areas and lead to learning problems. Consequently, strengthening of the ego or improving an inappropriate self-concept is likely to influence favorably numerous specific attitudes and patterns of overt behavior.

A successful remedial reading program (Keating, 1962), planned to improve the reading ability of boys eleven years and older in a Special School who were unable to read or who read too poorly to fit into a regular class, included the following features:

1] Twenty boys, ages twelve years, seven months, to fifteen years, four months, I.Q.'s of 60 to 93, with median of 75, reading retardation of eight months to nine years five months, were placed in groups of five and spent one period—one-fourth of the school day—in a "small, cosily-furnished sitting room" equipped with four cubicles in which the boys worked between personal conferences largely on self-checking material.

2] Each boy had the undivided attention of the teacher for fifteen to twenty minutes a day. During this period of individual attention he read a book, carefully selected with reference to his ability and interest, with the teacher who promptly supplied words whenever necessary. In some cases, the teacher wrote a book specially for a particular boy. Other methods were used whenever the boy needed them: phonics, "look-say," copy-writing exercises, sentence building with word cards, card-matching exercises, flash-card drill, and simple comprehension exercises.

3] For the remainder of the time, the boys worked on silent reading exercises or other activities designed to improve their reading.

4] Each boy had plenty of reading practice at his level.

5] Each boy wrote vocabulary cards of words on a standard frequency list and words with which he had difficulty. These vocabulary cards he carried about with him in a box and frequently reviewed and tested himself on them.

6]   An intimate person-to-person relationship was substituted for a classroom atmosphere.

7]   Attention was given to emotional factors such as feelings of inferiority, lack of self-confidence, and motivation, boredom, etc.

The results of this individualized program were superior to the usual remedial class procedure. Six of the twenty boys returned to a normal class with reading ages of ten to eleven years. Two left the school and eleven were accepted for continuation the following term with a good chance of success. However, the I.Q.'s of the boys in the individualized program were considerably higher than those of the boys in the remedial class.

Both the mental-health approach and practice and instruction in certain mental abilities underlying reading achievement were employed by Krippner (1964) with two groups of clinic cases. Since the subjects' scores on the WISC Performance Scale were higher than those on the WISC Verbal Scale, the plan of treatment was to capitalize on the client's non-verbal ability while improving his inadequate verbal ability. The treatment consisted of bibliotherapy, non-directive play therapy, "rational emotive counseling," and parent conferences. The clients were also given practice with the Fernald method, the Radaker Visual Imagery Technique, the Leavell eye-hand coordinator and, when appropriate, the Delacato stereo-reader. To improve perceptual skills, sandpaper letters, a "touch board," and Izzy cards were used and home exercises suggested for parent use.

A follow-up of the first group showed a change from a reading grade of 1.13 before attending the clinic to a mean grade of 2.04 during the following year. Significant relationships were found between reading improvement and total percentile on the Mental Health Analysis ($n = .46$, $p = .01$) and WISC Verbal I.Q. ($r = .44$, $p = .05$). The mean improvement in reading was .88 of a grade.

In the clinic the following year more emphasis was placed on utilizing non-verbal abilities and upon improving health. This time the forty subjects made a mean reading grade improvement of .89 according to the California Reading Test data, but the standard deviation was .74 and the range wide. Only one correlation proved to be statistically significant, that between reading improvement and the WISC Performance I.Q. (r = .33, p = .05). If more specific reading instruction had been given along with the other methods, the gains in reading might have been considerably higher. Other research has shown that while therapy alone produces gains in reading ability, a combination of reading instruction and therapy is the more effective.

The actual value of therapy in conjunction with remedial instruction is still under question. Results of several early investigations suggested significant gains in reading as a result of therapy. A more recent investigation showed no consistent effect due to psychotherapy (Schiffman, 1962). With cases in which causes of the disability are secondary, as defined by Rabinovitch (1962), a combination of therapy and remedial instruction is likely to be most effective.

From experience at Hawthorn Center, Rabinovitch stated:

> Equally evident was the fact that psychiatric treatment, especially of in-patients, could not be effective without concomitant reading therapy for many of our boys. So often the school social worker or pediatrician refers the child with the hope, and even expectation, that the psychiatric clinic will find the learning problem to be due to an "emotional block" and that through the magic of psychotherapy, perhaps limited to a few interviews, the child will be "released" to learn adequately. (1962, p. 73)

He went on to say:

> The problem is far more complex, and the understanding of the large mass of reading problems which we see represents, I believe, one of the major current challenges to our field. (1962, p. 74)

With reference to mild reading retardation secondary to emotional problems, Rabinovitch says that psychotherapy is indicated. For those with the primary or dyslexic syndrome, there is need for intensive long-term remedial therapy. "Our experience at Hawthorn indicates dramatically the need for early intervention as close to first-grade level as possible" (1962, pp. 78-79).

Part-time teachers in England, working with small groups

of retarded readers of junior school age, have obtained results fairly comparable to those of more elaborate remedial programs (Hillman & Snowdon, 1960). In addition to basic reading series, there were a large number of supplementary reading books. Although these teachers used a phonic rather than a whole-word or sentence-method approach, they felt free to develop their own ideas and to use methods they felt were appropriate to the individual children whom they were teaching.

Situations in which diagnosis and remediation may take place, to some extent, parallel the levels of diagnosis already described. The least recognized, and yet the most important, is the classroom level in which diagnosis is an intrinsic part of teaching. One degree removed from the regular classroom is the developmental reading course in which all students are given special instruction in reading. Somewhat more specialized is the remedial reading class to which retarded readers are referred. Serving a school system is the reading clinic where diagnostic studies are made. When staff is available, the diagnosis is followed by remedial work. Physically apart from the school system is the mental health clinic or psycholinguistic services set up in a hospital or university. Increasingly, individuals with reading problems are being referred for special diagnostic and treatment services.

If well qualified reading personnel are available, their time and services should be used to best advantage.

Severe reading disability, which may be due to a basic biological defect and is associated with emotional problems, is very difficult to correct and may require years of expert treatment. The law of diminishing returns for the effort expended is operating. Therefore, the reading specialist would accomplish far more by working with a much larger number of children who can improve quite readily in reading and with teachers who influence a still larger number of children And, although developmental reading should be taught on all educational levels, the reading specialist should include in his program pre-reading experiences for pre-school children and early diagnoses and remediation of kindergarten and first-grade children who show deficits in preception and other prerequisites for success in beginning reading.

Evaluation

The evaluation of remedial methods and programs is difficult and often depressing. It is difficult because the means of evaluation—usually standardized tests—may not measure some of the reading abilities and none of the attitudes and reading habits that may have been acquired. The task of keeping track of the initial group in a mobile population and the estimating of intervening influences are other problems of long-term evaluation. It is also very difficult to measure an individual's progress in reading in terms of his reading potential. Evaluation is often depressing because of the evidence of regression in ability after the stimulation of instruction has ceased. Yet any psychological clinic or school remedial program has the problem of evaluating the effectiveness of its service.

The usual methods of evaluation are: *1*] to follow-up students to ascertain their competence and progress in regular classes or schools after a period of time; *2*] to compare the progress made by the group receiving remedial instruction with a control group; and *3*] to compare individuals' achievement scores before and after treatment.

Little research is available on the long-term effect of remedial instruction. There is some evidence that remedial work is much more effective with initially able students than with severe cases of reading disability. An encouraging report came from a follow-up study of clients who had attended The University of Chicago Reading Clinic (Robinson & Smith, 1962). These were, for the most part, initially able students who had had reading difficulties in 1948. Of the 44 clients in the study, after ten years, only three had not completed high school; more than half had completed college; only one was neither attending college nor employed at the time the follow-up study was made.

Of 555 pupils from the St. Louis Public Schools Reading Clinic who had been diagnosed as cases of severe reading disability, seventy per cent graduated from elementary school and twenty per cent from high school (Adams, 1960). Remedial instruction, while resulting in a rise in reading quotient during the periods of instruction, tended to cease when the teaching was discontinued. The special instruction was not able to raise the backward readers to a higher level in their schools: "After a mean period of almost three and one-half years from the time of referral, no difference in the mean reading age could be found between those who did, and those who did not attend the remedial centers" (Lovell, Byrne, & Richardson, 1963, p. 9). Few children, backward at eight and one-half to nine years, were later found among the academically able pupils. Possible explanations of this lack of progress are: *1*] poor remedial methods, *2*] lack of carry-over from the remedial to the regular classes, *3*] a stigma attached to being in the remedial reading center, and *4*] home expectations that these children would remain in their initial and family status. Although the progress made by the majority of children in this study was small, it was of great importance to those who did attain a reading age of nine-plus years.

English children who had had remedial education were followed up one or two years after they had left the remedial group (Lytton, 1967). Some children lost some of their original reading gains over this period, but others maintained a large part of their gains, especially in reading, after remedial reading teaching ceased.

Twenty-five children with severe reading disability, initially studied at the Bellevue Hospital Mental Hygiene Clinic, were found twelve years later as young adults to still have psychological signs of specific problems of visual and tactile perception (Silver & Hagin, 1963). Those who initially had only psychological signs of neurological involvement showed greater improvement in reading than those who had organic signs.

The follow-up study by Balow and Blomquist (1965) suggests that life experiences as well as special instruction may lead to improvement in reading. A group of thirty-two elementary boys within the average range of intelligence and with an initial reading level two to five years below age-grade expectation were diagnosed as severely disabled readers at the University of Minnesota Psycho-Educational Clinic. After ten to fifteen intervening years, despite only sporadic instruction in reading throughout their elementary and secondary school years, had in some way learned to read at approximatley the average adult level (Balow & Blomquist, 1965). Most of them (83 per cent) had graduated from high school, and more than half had gone on to post-high school, vocational, and college education. None were unemployed. Their attitudes and interests, however, reflected their early reading disability: they did not like school; they did not read for pleasure or interest; they showed mild emotional disorders; they had a "slightly defeatist attitude toward life in general" (Balow & Blomquist, 1965, p. 48). They attributed their improvement in reading to their own efforts, not to the schools or teachers. Although initial reading ability and intelligence were taken into account and attempts made to obtain both subjective and objective evidence, there were still unanswered questions.

The case-study approach to evaluation is the only adequate way in which all the related factors that may influence an individual's subsequent achievement and adjustment can be evaluated.

7. Trends, needs, future directions

Although the importance of diagnosis has long been recognized, it has too often been considered an end in itself rather than a means of improving reading. Tests have been given and scored; statistics applied. But the results of all this work too seldom filtered down to the classroom teacher, and if it did, little use was made of it. Individual diagnostic studies were made of children referred to clinics, and more or less elaborate reports were sent to the schools. But, again, teachers were often not able to make connections between the diagnosis and the instruction they gave under classroom conditions.

There are straws in the wind that indicate an increased recognition of the close relationship between the information obtained through a diagnostic study of an individual or class and methods of teaching. There is general agreement that there is *no* one best method. The remedial method used should stem specifically from the diagnosis.

There is a growing emphasis on differential diagnosis of reading achievement. By analyzing the components of the reading process, it is possible to plan more specific remediation.

Another important discernible trend is represented by the behavioral approach:

> The very fact that we cannot exchange parents or repair damaged brains has led to the present-day concern of many with behavioral and symptomatic rather than pathological or etiological factors. (Bateman, 1965, p. 168)

Since definite correlations of brain pathology with reading disability have not been established, remediation must still be planned on the basis of observed behavior.

Most progress has been made in the areas of perception and perceptual-motor abilities. Visual perception has been thoroughly analyzed, and tests based on extensive research have been developed. The work of de Hirsch, Frostig, and Wepman are outstanding examples. Auditory perception, discrimination, and memory have been similarly studied by Wepman and others. The next step is the thorough study of the integration of visual and auditory perception. This has been done in the Illinois Test of Psycholinguistic Abilities which diagnoses the reading process from intake to output—a most important development in the field of diagnostic testing of reading.

Although these new instruments are of great value for differential diagnosis, the emphasis, unfortunately, seems to be more on prediction than on diagnosis. The tests of visual and auditory perception and perceptual-motor abilities are recommended for use in screening pre-school, kindergarten, and first-grade children to determine whether they are good or poor risks for beginning reading instruction. There is need for a follow-up of these predictions with diagnostic teaching in which the specific strengths and weaknesses revealed by the tests will be recognized, utilized, and remedied in the classroom.

There has also been much interest in studying the relation of mental abilities as measured by sub-tests of the WISC and the WAIS to reading achievement. If these underlying abilities could be strengthened, improvement in reading might be expected.

Some attention is being increasingly given to ascertaining the individual's preferred avenues of learning. Research has shown that some individuals on different age levels prefer the whole versus the part approach; others, the auditory versus the visual, and vice versa. It is recommended that the teacher recognize these different modalities and use the methods by which individual children learn most readily. At the same time, it may be possible to strengthen the modality in which they are weak.

This policy is part of a larger controversial theory of diagnosis—whether in general to build on whatever strengths are available and ignore the weak aspects or to concentrate on correcting faults and deflecting fault lines. Again, it is not "either-or." The teacher or clinician will begin instruction with what the individual can do best. This will give him courage and encouragement. Then as he comes to recognize the need for correcting errors and overcoming difficulties, he will be receptive to specific instruction.

Increased emphasis on early diagnosis is another trend that is being made possible by the newer tests of visual and auditory perception. As in child development in general, much more research is now being carried on with pre-school, kindergarten, and first-grade children than with children in the intermediate and secondary grades.

Important as it is to get off to a good start, the sequential development of reading abilities at each age into adulthood is also essential. Diagnosis of the later developmental reading stages has been seriously neglected. Reading tests still do not give reliable and valid information on the higher reading skills of interpretation, critical reading, and ability to comprehend the author's pattern of thought simultaneously with the reading. There is need for analysis of the reading process on these higher levels, comparable to studies that have recently been made with pre-school children.

Research on eye movements has definitely subsided, and fewer remedial programs using machines exclusively have recently been described.

Research on the diagnostic process itself is practically non-existent. There is little evidence that the recommended remedial techniques, if used, would be effective, or that techniques not recommended would get equally good results. What evidence there is depends upon the extensive research on the relationship of the numerous correlates and causes to reading achievement. An indefinite number of individuals may show the psychological responses characteristic of retarded readers and yet have no obvious reading difficulty. There is no proof that the "shotgun method" of trying many different procedures, as many remedial reading teachers do, does not result in reading improvement. Research along this line would be difficult to design because of all the uncontrolled variables that might influence the individual's progress.The gains may be related to the personality of the teacher, to the individual's modified value system, to the parents' change in attitude, or to innumerable other factors. Research would also be difficult because diagnosis is an evolving process. Any initial diagnostic formulation is modified as work with the individual or the remedial group continues; a diagnosis cannot be made once and for all.

In view of this complexity and continuity of the diagnostic process, more research should be of an intensive case-study type. This would make it possible to study the sequence of diagnosis and remediation within an individual each having a reciprocal relationship to the other over a period of time. The effort that would have to be expended on the construction of comprehensive test batteries might be used in developing teacher's and clinician's skill in observing children's and adolescents' behavior and in learning to respond to it with appropriate teaching and guidance procedures.

A less idealistic suggestion for future direction is to extract more diagnostic information from the best diagnostic instruments and from other sources of information about correlates and causes now available. By analyzing the test responses with the students and suggesting ways in which correct answers can be obtained and errors avoided, the teacher uses the test as a teaching as well as a diagnostic device.

Finally, much more emphasis should be placed on self-diagnosis. Students should be given instruction and practice in self-appraisal leading to improvement in all aspects of reading. Introspective and retrospective verbalization as a diagnostic technique should be developed. Both students and teachers participate in the process of self-appraisal—students with respect to their own reading; teachers with respect to their methods of teaching reading.

Research on the efficacy of teaching procedures with certain individuals under certain conditions would provide a background of understanding and a repertory of diagnostic and teaching methods and materials from which teachers and clinicians could select those most appropriate for the individuals or groups with whom they are working.

REFERENCES

Ackerman, N. W. A plan for maladjusted children. *The Menninger Foundation*, 1936, *1*, 310.

Adams, Mary L. The St. Louis public schools reading clinics: a follow-up study. Unpublished doctoral dissertation, St. Louis University, 1960.

Alexander, D., & Money, J. Reading ability, object constancy, and Turner's syndrome. *Perceptual and Motor Skills*, 1965, *20*, 981-84.

Anapolle, L. Visual training and reading performance. *Journal of Reading*, 1967, *10*, 372-82.

Ausubel, D. P., & Fitzgerald, D. The role of discriminability in meaningful verbal learning and retention. *Journal of Educational Psychology*, 1961, *52*, 366-74.

Baker, M. J., & Leland, Bernice. *Detroit test of learning aptitude.* Indianapolis: Bobbs Merrill Co., 1935-55.

Balow, B., & Blomquist, M. Young adults ten to fifteen years after severe reading disability. *Elementary School Journal*, 1965, *66*, 44-48.

Balow, I. H. Lateral dominance characteristics and reading achievement in the first grade. *Journal of Psychology*, 1963, *55*, 323-28.

Barclay, G. L. i/t/a with emotionally disturbed children. In F. B. Davis (Ed.), Modern educational developments: another look. *Thirtieth Educational Conference of the Educational Records Bureau*, 1966, *30*, 135-46.

Bateman, Barbara. *The Illinois test of psycholinguistic abilities in current research: summaries of studies.* Urbana, Ill.: University of Illinois Press, 1965.

Bateman, Barbara. Learning disorders. *Review of Educational Research*, 1966, *36*, 93-119.

Bateman, Barbara. Learning disabilities, yesterday, today, and tomorrow. *Exceptional Children*, 1965, *31*, 167-77.

Bell, R., & Schaefer, E. The parental attitude research instrument. *National Institute of Mental Health*, U. S. Department of Health, Education, and Welfare, 1957.

Belmont, Lillian, & Birch, H. G. Lateral dominance, lateral awareness, and reading disability. *Child Development*, 1965, *36*, 57-71.

Bender, Lauretta. *Bender visual motor Gestalt test.* New York: The Psychological Corporation, 1946.

Bender, Lauretta. Problems in conceptualization and communication in children with developmental alexia. In P. H. Hoch & J. Zubin (Eds.), *Psychopathology of communication.* New York: Grune & Stratton, 1958. Pp. 155-76.

Benton, A. L. Dyslexia in relation to form perception and directional sense. In J. Money (Ed.), *Reading disability: progress in research needs in dyslexia.* Baltimore: John Hopkins Press, 1962. Pp. 81-102.

Benton, A. L., & Bird, J. W. The EEG and reading disability. *American Journal of Orthopsychiatry,* 1963, *33,* 529-31.

Birch, H. G., & Belmont, Lillian, Auditory-visual integration in normal and retarded readers. *American Journal of Orthopsychiatry,* 1964, *34,* 852-61.

Birch, H. G., & Belmont, Lillian. Auditory-visual integration, intelligence, and reading ability in school children. *Perceptual and Motor Skills,* 1965, *20,* 295-305.

Blanchard, Phyllis. Reading disabilities in relation to maladjustment. *Mental Hygiene,* 1928, *12,* 772-88.

Bliesmer, E. P. A comparison of results of various capacity tests used with retarded readers. *Elementary School Journal,* 1956, *56,* 400-02.

Bloomer, R. H. Investigations of an experimental first-grade phonics program. *Journal of Educational Research,* 1960, *53,* 188-93.

Bloomer, R. H. The cloze procedure as a remedial reading exercise. *Journal of Developmental Reading,* 1962, *5,* 173-81.

Bollenbacker, Joan. A study of the effect of mobility on reading achievement. *The Reading Teacher,* 1962, *15,* 356-60.

Bond, G. L., & Tinker, M. A. *Reading difficulties: their diagnosis and correction.* (2nd ed.) New York. Appleton-Century-Crofts, 1967.

Bormuth, J. R. Mean word depth as a predictor of comprehension difficulty. *California Journal of Educational Research,* 1964, *15,* 226-31.

Bormuth, J. R. Comparable cloze and multiple-choice comprehension test scores. *Journal of Reading,* 1967, *10,* 291-99.

Boshes, B., & Myklebust, H. R. A neurological and behavioral study of children with learning disorders. *Neurology,* 1964, *14,* 7-12.

Bower, E. M. *Early identification of emotionally handicapped children in school.* Springfield, Ill.: Charles C. Thomas, 1960.

Bowers, J. E. Study of children with unusual difficulty in reading and arithmetic. *Canadian Education and Research Digest,* 1964, *4,* 273-78.

Brown, J. I., & Carlsen, G. R. *Brown-Carlsen listening comprehension test: evaluation and adjustment series.* New York: Harcourt, Brace, and World, Inc., 1953-55.

Brzeinski, J. E. Beginning reading in Denver. *The Reading Teacher,* 1964, *18,* 16-21.

Budoff, M., & Quinlan, D. Reading progress as related to difficulty of visual and aural learning in the primary grades. *Journal of Educational Psychology,* 1964, *55,* 247-52.

Burnett, R. W. The diagnostic proficiency of teachers of reading. *The Reading Teacher,* 1963, *16,* 229-39.

Buros, O. K. (Ed.) *The sixth mental measurements yearbook.* Highland Park, N. J.: Gryphon Press, 1965.

Capobianco, R. J. Ocular-manual laterality and reading in adolescent mental retardates. *American Journal of Mental Deficiency,* 1966, *70,* 781-85.

Carrithers, Lura M. Beginning reading patterns and pre-school emotional problems. *Educational Horizons,* 1965, *44,* 3-9.

Cawley, J. F. Reading performance among the mentally handicapped: a problem of assessment. *The Training School Bulletin,* 1966, *63,* 11-16.

Challman, Robert C. Personality maladjustments and remedial reading. *Journal of Exceptional Children,* 1939, *6,* 7-11.

Chang, T. M. C., & Chang, Vivian. Relation of visual-motor skills and reading achievement in primary-grade pupils of superior ability. *Perceptual and Motor Skills,* 1967, *24,* 51-53.

Chansky, N. M. Perceptual training with elementary school underachievers. *Journal of School Psychology,* 1963, *1*(1), 33-41. (a)

Chansky, N. M. Age, I.Q. and improvement of reading. *Journal of Educational Research,* 1963, *56,* 439. (b)

Clawson, Aileen. *Bender visual Gestalt test for children.* Beverly Hills, Calif.: Western Psychological Services, 1962.

Cline, M., Jr. A-V aids for Spanish-speaking pupils. In J. A. Figurel (Ed.), Reading and inquiry. *Conference Proceedings of the International Reading Association,* 1965, *10,* 270-71.

Cohn, R. Neurological concepts pertaining to the brain-damaged child. In W. T. Daley (Ed.), *Speech and language therapy with the brain-damaged child.* Washington, D. C.: Catholic University of America Press, 1962.

Cohn, R. The neurological study of children with learning disabilities. *Exceptional Children,* 1964, *31,* 179-85.

Coleman, J. C., & Rasof, Beatrice. Intellectual factors in learning disorders. *Perceptual and Motor Skills,* 1963, *16,* 139-52.

Coleman, R. I., & Deutsch, Cynthia P. Lateral dominance and right-left discrimination: a comparison of normal and retarded readers. *Perceptual and Motor Skills,* 1964, *19,* 43-50.

Committee on Diagnostic Reading Tests. *Diagnostic reading tests, survey section, auditory comprehension.* Mountain Home, N. C.: Author, 1957-63.

Cowen, E. L., Zax, M., & Klein, R. The relation of anxiety in school children to school record, achievement, and behavioral measures. *Child Development,* 1965, *36,* 685-93.

Cromer, W., & Wiener, M. Idiosyncratic response patterns among good and poor readers. *Journal of Consulting Psychology,* 1966, *30,* 1-10.

Cruickshank, W. M., Bentzen, Frances A., Ratzeburg, F. H., & Tannhauser, Miriam. *A teaching method for brain-injured and hyperactive children: a demonstration pilot study.* Syracuse, N. Y.: Syracuse University Press, 1961.

Curr, W., & Gourlay, N. D. The effect of practice on performance in scholastic tests. *British Journal of Educational Psychology,* 1960, *30,* 155-67.

Daly, W. C., & Lee, R. H. Reading disabilities in a group of m-r children: incidence and treatment. *Training School Bulletin,* 1960, *57,* 85-93.

Davy, Ruth A. Adaptations of progressive choice method for teaching reading to retarded children. *American Journal of Mental Deficiency,* 1962, *67,* 274-80.

de Hirsch, Katrina. Concepts related to normal reading processes and their application to reading pathology. *Journal of Genetic Psychology,* 1963, *102,* 277-85.

de Hirsch, Katrina, Jansky, Jeannette J., and Langford, W. S. *Predicting reading failure.* New York: Harper and Row, 1966.

Deutsch, Cynthia P. Auditory discrimination and learning: social factors. *Merrill-Palmer Quarterly of Behavior and Development,* 1964, *10,* 277-96.

Dubnoff, Belle. Excerpts from "perceptual training as a bridge to conceptual ability." *Los Angeles City School Districts Division of Elementary Education,* 1966, 1-10. (Reprinted from *Educational Therapy* by permission of Special Child Publications of the Sequin School, Inc., Seattle, Washington.)

Duker, S. *Listening: readings.* New York: Scarecrow Press, 1966.

Duker, S. Listening. *Review of Educational Research,* 1964, *34,* 156-62.

Dunham, J. IV-The effects of remedial education on young children's reading ability and attitude to reading. *British Journal of Educational Psychology,* 1960, *30,* 173-75.

Dunn, J. A. Inter- and intra-rater reliability of the new Harris-Goodenough draw-a-man test. *Perceptual and Motor Skills,* 1967, *24,* 269-70. (a)

Dunn, J. A. Validity coefficients for the new Harris-Goodenough draw-a-man test. *Perceptual and Motor Skills*, 1967, *24*, 299-301. (b)

Durkin, Dolores. Children who read before grade one: a second study. *Elementary School Journal*, 1963, *64*, 143-48.

Durrell, D., & Murphy, Helen A. The auditory discrimination factor in reading readiness and reading disability. *Education*, 1953, *73*, 556-60.

Dykstra, R. Auditory discrimination abilities and beginning reading achievement. *Reading Research Quarterly*. 1966, *1* (3), 5-34.

Eames, T. H. Visual handicaps to reading. *Journal of Education*, 1959, *141*, 1-35.

Eames, T. H. Some neural and glandular bases of learning. *Boston University Journal of Education*. 1960, *142* 3-36.

Eames, T. H. The effect of anisometropia on reading achievement. *American Journal of Optometry and Archives of American Academy of Optometry*, 1964, *41*, 700-02.

Educational Testing Service. *Sequential test of educational progress: listening*. Princeton, N. J.: Author, 1956-63.

Ekwall, E. E. The use of WISC sub-test profiles in the diagnosis of reading difficulties. Unpublished doctoral dissertation, University of Arizona, 1966.

Ephron, Beulah K. *Emotional difficulties in reading*. New York: Julian Press, 1953.

Epstein, W. Experimental investigations of the genesis of visual space perception. *Psychological Bulletin*, 1964, *61*, 115-28.

Evans, J. W., Jr. The effect of pupil mobility upon academic achievement. *National Elementary Principal*, 1966, *45* (5), 18-22.

Farnham-Diggory, Sylvia. Symbol and synthesis in experimental reading. *Child Development*, 1967, *38*, 221-31.

Fernald, Grace. *Remedial techniques in basic school subjects*. New York: McGraw-Hill, 1943.

Flower, R. M., Gofman, Helen F., & Lawson, Lucie I. (Eds.) *Reading disorders*. Philadelphia: F. A. Davis, 1965.

Flower, R. M., Viehweg, R., & Ruzieka, W. R. The communicative disorders of children with kernicteric athetosis: problems in language comprehension and use. *Journal of Speech and Hearing Disorders*, 1966, *31*, 60-68.

Fowler, W. A study of process and method in three-year-old twins and triplets learning to read. *Genetic Psychology Monographs*, 1965, *72*, 3-89.

Fransella, Fay, & Gerver, D. Multiple regression equations for predicting reading age from chronological age and WISC verbal I.Q. *British Journal of Educational Research*, 1965, *11*, 167-75.

French, J. L. *Pictorial test of intelligence*. Boston: Houghton Mifflin, 1964. P. 134.

Frost, B. P. Intelligence, manifest anxiety, and scholastic achievement. *Alberta Journal of Educational Research*, 1965, *11*, 167-75.

Frost, B. P. The role of intelligence "C" in the selection of children for remedial teaching of reading. *Alberta Journal of Educational Research*, 1963, *9*, 73-78.

Frostig, Marianne, Lefever, D. W., & Whittlesey, J. A developmental test of visual perception for evaluating normal and neurologically handicapped children. *Perceptual and Motor Skills*, 1961, *12*, 383-94.

Frostig, Marianne, Lefever, D. W., Whittlesey, J., & Maslow, Phyllis. *Marianne Frostig developmental test of visual perception*. Palo Alto, Calif.: Consulting Psychologist Press, 1961-64.

Fuller, G. B., & Laird, J. T. The Minnesota Percepto-Diagnostic Test. *Journal of Clinical Psychology, Monograph Supplement*, 1963, *16*, 1-33.

Gallagher, J. J. *The tutoring of brain-injured mentally retarded children*. Springfield, Ill.: Charles C. Thomas, 1960.

Gallagher, J. J. Changes in verbal and non-verbal ability of brain-injured mentally retarded children following removal of special stimulation. *American Journal of Mental Deficiency*, 1962, *66*, 774-81. (a)

Gallagher, J. J. Educational methods with brain-damaged children. In J. H. Masserman (Ed.), *Current psychiatric therapies*. Vol. 2. New York: Grune & Stratton, 1962. (b)

Gates, A. I. *The Gates reading readiness tests*. New York: Bureau of Publications, Teachers College, Columbia University, 1939-42.

Geake, R. R. Predictors of reading improvement. In *Inter-institutional Seminar in Child Development, Collected Papers*. Dearborn, Michigan: Edison Institute, 1963. Pp. 86-93.

Gibson, Eleanor J., Bishop, Carol H., Schiff, W., & Smith, Jesse. Comparison of meaningfulness and pronunciability as grouping principles in the perception and retention of verbal material. *Journal of Experimental Psychology*, 1964, *67*, 173-82.

Gibson, Eleanor J., Gibson, J. J., Pick, Anne D., & Osser, H. A developmental study of the discrimination of letter-like forms. *Journal of Comparative and Physiological Psychology*, 1962, *55*, 897-906.

Gifford, Edith M., & Marston, A. P. Test anxiety, reading rate, and task experience. *Journal of Educational Research*, 1966, *59*, 303-06.

Gilbert, L. C. Genetic study of eye movements in reading. *Elementary School Journal,* 1959, *59,* 328-35.

Gillingham, Anna, & Stillman, Bessie W. *Remedial training for children with specific disability in reading, spelling, and penmanship.* New York: Sackett and Wilhelms Lithographing Corp., 1940.

Goins, Jean T. Visual perceptual abilities and early reading progress. *University of Chicago Supplemental Educational Monographs,* 1958, No. 87.

Goodenough, Florence, & Harris, D. B. *Children's drawing as measures of intellectual maturity: a revision and extension of the Goodenough draw-a-man test.* New York: Harcourt, Brace, & World, 1963.

Graham, E. E., & Kamano, D. Reading failure as a factor in the WAIS sub-test patterns of youthful offenders. *Journal of Clinical Psychology,* 1958, *14,* 302-05.

Gruber, E. Reading ability, binocular coordination, and the ophthalmograph. *Archives of Ophthalmology,* 1962, *67,* 280-88.

Haberland, J. A. A comparison of listening tests with standardized tests. *Journal of Educational Research,* 1959, *52,* 299-302.

Hafner, L. E. (Ed.) *Improving reading in secondary schools.* New York: Macmillan, 1967.

Hage, D. S., & Stroud, J. B. Reading proficiency and intelligence scores, verbal and non-verbal. *Journal of Educational Research,* 1959, *52,* 258-62.

Hagin, Rosa A., Silver, A. A., & Hersh, Marilyn F. Specific reading disability: teaching by stimulation of deficit perceptual areas. In J. A. Figurel (Ed.), Reading and inquiry. *Proceedings of the International Reading Association,* 1965, *10,* 368-70.

Haring, N. G., & Ridgway, R. W. Early identification of children with learning disabilities. *Exceptional Children,* 1967, *33,* 387-95.

Harris, A. J. *Harris tests of lateral dominance.* New York: Psychological Corp., 1947-58.

Harris, A. J. *How to increase reading ability: a guide to developmental and remedial methods.* (4th ed.) New York: Longmans, Green & Co., 1961.

Harrison, Lucille, & Stroud, J. B. *The Harrison-Stroud reading readiness profiles.* Boston: Houghton Mifflin, 1949-56.

Harvey, O. J. (Ed.) *Experience, structure, and adaptability.* New York: Springer Publishing Co., 1966.

Haspiel, G. S., & Bloomer, R. H. Maximum auditory perception (MAP) word list. *Journal of Speech and Hearing Disorders,* 1961, *26,* 156-63.

Hegge, G., Kirk, S. A., & Kirk, Winifred D. *Remedial reading drills, with directions by Samuel A. Kirk.* Ann Arbor, Mich.: George Wahr Publishing Co., 1955.

Hermann, K. Congenital word-blindness. *ACTA psychiatrica et neurologica, Scandinavica Supplementum,* 108. Copenhagen: Universitetsforlaget 1 Aarhus, 1956.

Hewett, F. M., Mayhew, D., & Rabb, Ethel. An experimental reading program for neurologically impaired, mentally retarded, and severely emotionally disturbed children. *American Journal of Orthopsychiatry,* 1967, *37,* 35-48.

Hill, E. H., & Giammatteo, M. C. Socio-economic status and its relation to school achievement in the elementary school. *Elementary English,* 1963, *40,* 265-70.

Hillerich, R. L. Interpretation of research in reading readiness. *Elementary English,* 1966, *43,* 359-64.

Hillman, H. H., and Snowdon, R. L. III-part-time classes for young backward readers. *British Journal of Educational Psychology,* 1960, *30,* 168-72.

Hirst, Lynne. The usefulness of a two-way analysis of WISC sub-tests in the diagnosis of remedial reading problems. *Journal of Experimental Education,* 1960, *29,* 153-60.

Hobbs, N. Helping disturbed children: psychological and ecological strategies. *American Psychologist,* 1966, *21,* 1105-15.

Holmes, J. A. Personality characteristics of the disabled reader. *Journal of Developmental Reading,* 1961, *4,* 111-22.

Holmes, J. A., & Singer, H. *The substrata factor theory: substrata factor differences underlying reading ability in known groups on the high school level.* Berkeley: University of California, 1961.

Horowitz, M. W., & Berkowitz, A. Listening and reading, speaking and writing: an experimental investigation of differential acquisition and reproduction of memory. *Perceptual and Motor Skills,* 1967, *24,* 207-15.

Huelsman, C. B. Some recent research on visual problems in reading. *American Journal of Optometry and Archives of American Academy of Optometry Monograph,* 1959, No. 240.

Hutt, M. L., & Briskin, G. J. *Bender revised Gestalt test.* New York: Grune & Stratton, Inc., 1960.

Jones, J. K. Colour as an aid to visual perception in early reading. *British Journal of Educational Psychology,* 1965, *35,* 21-27.

Kass, Corrine E. Psycholinguistic disabilities of children with reading problems. *Exceptional Children,* 1966, *32,* 533-39.

Katz, Phyllis A., & Deutsch, M. Modality of stimulus presentation in serial learning for retarded and normal readers. *Perceptual and Motor Skills,* 1964, *19,* 627-33.

Kawi, A. A., & Pasamanick, B. Prenatal and paranatal factors in the development of childhood reading disorders. *Monograph of the Society for Research in Child Development,* 1959, *24,* 2-80.

Keating, L. E. A pilot experiment in remedial reading at the hospital school, Lingfield, 1957-1960. *British Journal of Educational Psychology,* 1962, *32,* 62-65.

Kelley, Marjorie L., & Chen, M. K. An experimental study of formal reading instruction at the kindergarten level. *Journal of Educational Research,* 1967, *60,* 224-29.

Keogh, Barbara K. The Bender Gestalt as a predictive and diagnostic test of reading performance. *Journal of Consulting Psychology,* 1965, *29,* 83-84.

Kephart, N. C. Perceptual-motor problems of children. *Proceedings of the Conference on Exploration into the Problems of the Perceptually Handicapped Child,* 1963, *6,* 27-30.

King, Ethel M., & Muehl, S. Different sensory cues as aids in beginning reading. *The Reading Teacher,* 1965, *19,* 163-68.

Kirk, S. A. Reading problems of slow learners. In H. A. Robinson (Ed.), The underachiever in reading. *University of Chicago Supplementary Educational Monographs,* 1962, No. 92.

Kirk, S. A., & McCarthy, J. J. The Illinois Test of Psycholinguistic Abilities—an approach to differential diagnosis. *American Journal of Mental Deficiency,* 1961, *66,* 399-412.

Koppitz, Elizabeth M. *Bender Gestalt test for young children.* New York: Grune & Stratton, Inc., 1964.

Koppitz, Elizabeth M., Mardis, V., & Stephens, T. A note on screening school beginners with the Bender Gestalt test. *Journal of Educational Psychology,* 1961, *52,* 80-81.

Krippner, S. Diagnostic and remedial use of the Minnesota Percepto-Diagnostic Test in a reading clinic. *Psychology in the Schools,* 1966, *3,* 171-75. (a)

Krippner, S. Reading improvement and scores on the Holtzman Inkblot Technique. *The Reading Teacher,* 1966, *19,* 519-22. (b)

Krippner, S., & Herald, Clara. Reading disabilities among the academically talented. *Gifted Child Quarterly,* 1964, *8,* 12-20.

Kucera, O., Matejcek, Z., & Langmeier, J. Some observations on dyslexia in children in Czechoslavakia. *American Journal of Orthopsychiatry,* 1963, *33,* 448-56.

Lawson, J. R., & Avils, D. Comparison of wide-range achievement test and Gray oral reading paragraphs reading scores of mentally retarded adults. *Perceptual and Motor Skills,* 1962, *14,* 474.

Lee, J. M., & Clark, W. W. *The Lee-Clark reading readiness test.* Monterey, Calif.: Test Bureau, 1963.

Leibert, R. E. An investigation of the differences in reading performance on two tests of reading. Unpublished doctoral dissertation, Syracuse University, 1965.

Lennon, R. T. What can be measured? *The Reading Teacher,* 1962, *15,* 326-27.

Leton, D. A. Visual-motor capacities and ocular efficiency in reading. *Perceptual and Motor Skills,* 1962, *15,* 407-32.

Lipsitt, L. P. A self-concept scale for children and its relationship to the children's form of the Manifest Anxiety Scale. *Child Development,* 1958, *29,* 463-72.

Livengood, Dorothy. The effect of bibliotherapy upon peer relations and democratic practices in a sixth-grade classroom. Unpublished doctoral dissertation, University of Florida, 1961.

Long, Roberta, A. A printed materials-centered approach compared with a machine-centered approach for improving the reading efficiency of college students. Unpublished doctoral dissertation, University of Oklahoma, 1962.

Lovell, K., Byrne, C., & Richardson, B. A further study of the educational progress of children who had received remedial education. *British Journal of Educational Psychology,* 1963, *33,* 3-9.

Lovell, K., Gray, E. A., & Oliver, D. E. A further study of some cognitive and other disabilities in backward readers of average non-verbal reasoning scores. *British Journal of Educational Psychology,* 1964, *34,* 275-79.

Lovell, K., Johnson, E., & Platts, D. A summary of a study of the reading ages of children who had been given remedial reading. *British Journal of Educational Psychology,* 1962, *32,* 66-71.

Lovell, K., Shapton, D., & Warren, N. S. A study of some cognitive and other disabilities in backward readers of average intelligence as assessed by a non-verbal test. *British Journal of Educational Psychology,* 1964, *34,* 58-64.

Lovell, K., & Woolsey, M. E. Reading disability, non-verbal, reasoning, and social class. *British Journal of Educational Research,* 1964, *6,* 226-27.

Lundsteen, Sara W. Teaching abilities in critical listening in fifth and sixth grades. Unpublished doctoral dissertation, University of California at Berkeley, 1963.

Lundsteen, Sara W. Teaching and testing critical listening in fifth and sixth grades. *Elementary English,* 1964, *41,* 743-47.

Lytton, H. Follow-up of an experiment in selection for remedial education. *British Journal of Educational Psychology,* 1967, *37,* 1-9.

Lytton, H. Symposium: contributions to the diagnosis and remedial treatment of reading difficulties. VI—An experiment in selection for remedial education. *British Journal of Educational Psychology,* 1961, *31,* 79-94.

MacDonald, Dorothy P. An investigation of the attitudes of parents of unsuccessful and successful readers. *Journal of Educational Research,* 1963, *56,* 437-38.

Malmquist, E. Factors related to reading disabilities in the first grade. In *Stockholm Studies in Educational Psychology.* Stockholm: Almquist and Wikseil, 1960. Pp. 1-428.

Marchbanks, Gabrielle, and Levin, H. Cues by which children recognize words. *Journal of Educational Psychology,* 1965, *56,* 57-61.

Maslow, Phyllis, Frostig, Marianne, Lefever, D. W., & Whittlesey, J. R. The Marianne Frostig developmental test of visual perception, 1963 standardization. *Perceptual and Motor Skills,* 1964, *19,* 463-99.

McCarthy, J. J., & Kirk, S. A. *The Illinois test of psycholinguistic abilities.* (Experimental Ed.) Urbana: University of Illinois Press, 1961-63.

McCarthy, J. J., & Kirk, S. A. *The construction, standardization, and statistical characteristics of the Illinois Test of Psycholinguistic Abilities.* Urbana: University of Illinois Press, 1963.

McCracken, R. A. Standardized reading tests and informal reading inventories. *Education,* 1962, *82,* 366-69.

McDonald, A. S. Factors affecting reading test performance. In Research and evaluation in college reading. *Ninth Yearbook of the National Reading Conference,* 1960, *9,* 28-35.

McDonald, A. S. What current research says about poor readers in high school and college. *Journal of Developmental Reading,* 1961, *4,* 184-96.

McDonald, A. S., Zolik, E. S., & Byrne, J. A. Reading deficiencies and personality factors: a comprehensive treatment. In Starting and improving college reading programs. *Eighth Yearbook of the National Reading Conference,* 1959, *8,* 89-98.

McMurray, J. G. Some correlates of reading difficulty in satisfactory and disabled readers: a preliminary study in grade 3. *Ontario Journal of Educational Research,* 1963, *5,* 149-57.

Mendenhall, G. V. *Analysis of differences between language and non-language I.Q.'s of the California test of mental maturity.* Los Angeles: California Test Bureau, 1959.

Minuchin, S., Chamberlain, Pamela, & Graubard, P. A project to teach learning skills to disturbed, delinquent children. *American Journal of Orthopsychiatry,* 1967, *37,* 558-67.

Money, J. Dyslexia: a post conference review. In J. Money (Ed.), *Read-*

ing disability: progress and research needs in dyslexia. Baltimore: Johns Hopkins Press, 1962. Chap. 1.

Money, J. (Ed.) *The disabled reader: education of the dyslexic child.* Baltimore: Johns Hopkins Press, 1966.

Monroe, Marian. *Reading aptitude tests: primary form.* Boston: Houghton Mifflin, 1935.

Monroe, Marian. *Children who cannot read.* Chicago: University of Chicago Press, 1946.

Moran, R. E. Levels of attainment of educable sub-normal adolescents. *British Journal of Educational Psychology,* 1960, *30,* 201-10.

Morton, J. The effects of context on the visual duration threshold for words. *British Journal of Psychology,* 1965, *55,* 165-80.

Myklebust, H. R., & Johnson, Doris. Dyslexia in children. *Exceptional Children,* 1962, *29,* 14-25.

Neal, Carolyn M. A study of the relationship of personality variables to reading ability utilizing tests administered to college freshmen. Unpublished doctoral dissertation, University of Illinois, 1964.

Neville, D. The relationship between reading skills and intelligence test scores. *The Reading Teacher,* 1965, *18,* 257-62.

Nichols, R., & Stevens, L. A. *Are you listening?* New York: McGraw-Hill, 1957.

Norman, R. D., & Daley, M. F. The comparative personality adjustment of superior and inferior readers. *Journal of Educational Psychology,* 1959, *50,* 31-36.

Pennema, Elizabeth N. Mental imagery and the reading process. *Elementary School Journal,* 1959, *59,* 286-89.

Penty, Ruth. *Reading ability and high school drop-outs.* New York: Teachers College Press, 1956.

Peters, Margaret L. The influence of reading methods on spelling. *British Journal of Educational Psychology,* 1967, *37,* 47-53.

Plessas, G. P., & Oakes, C. R. Pre-reading experiences of early readers. *The Reading Teacher,* 1964, *17,* 241-45.

Pronovost, W., & Dumbleton, C. A picture-type speech sound discrimination test. *Journal of Speech and Hearing Disorders,* 1953, *18,* 258-66.

Rabinovitch, R. D. Reading and learning disabilities. In S. Arieti (Ed.), *American handbook of psychiatry.* Vol. 1. New York: Basic Books, 1959. Pp. 857-69.

Rabinovitch, R. D. Dyslexia: psychiatric considerations. In J. Money

(Ed.), *Reading disability progress and research needs in dyslexia.*
Baltimore: Johns Hopkins Press, 1962. Pp. 72-79.

Rabinovitch, R. D. Educational achievement in children with psychiatric
problems. *Bulletin of the Orton Society,* 1964, *14,* 1-5.

Radaker, L. D. Imagery and academic performance. *Elementary School
Journal,* 1962, *63,* 91-95.

Ramsey, W. A study of salient characteristics of pupils of high and low
reading ability. *Journal of Developmental Reading,* 1962, *5,* 87-94.

Rankin, E. F., Jr. Reading test reliability and validity as function of
introversion-extroversion. *Journal of Developmental Reading,* 1963,
6, 106-17.

Raven, J. C. *Standard progressive matrices.* New York: Psychological
Corp., 1956.

Ravenette, A. T. VII—An empirical approach to the assessment of reading retardation: vocabulary level and reading attainment. *British
Journal of Educational Psychology,* 1961, *31,* 96-103.

Raygor, A. L., & Wark, R. M. Personality patterns of poor readers
compared with college freshmen. *Journal of Reading,* 1964, *8,*
40-46.

Reed, J. The relationship between the primary mental abilities and reading achievement at given developmental levels. *American Psychologist,* 1958, *7,* 324.

Reger, R. Reading ability and CMAS scores in educable mentally retarded
boys. *American Journal of Mental Deficiency,* 1964, *68,* 652-55.

Rhodes, W. C. The disturbing child: a problem of ecological manage-
ment. *Exceptional Children,* 1967, *33,* 449-55.

Richardson, J.A. Physical factors in reading failure. *Australian Journal
of Education,* 1958, *2,* 1-10.

Robeck, Mildred C. Children who show undue tension when reading: a
group diagnosis. In J. A. Figurel (Ed.), Challenge and experiment
in reading. *Proceedings of the International Reading Association,*
1962, *7,* 133-38.

Robeck, Mildred C. Effects of prolonged reading disability: a preliminary study. *Perceptual and Motor Skills,* 1964, *19,* 7-12.

Roberts, G. R. V—A study of motivation in remedial reading. *British
Journal of Educational Psychology,* 1960, *30,* 176-79.

Robertson, Jean E. An investigation of pupil understanding of connectives in reading. Unpublished doctoral dissertation, University of
Alberta, 1966.

Robinson, H. A. A study of the techniques of word identification. *The
Reading Teacher,* 1963, *16,* 238-42.

Robinson, Helen M. Diagnosis and treatment of poor readers with vision
problems. In Clinical studies in reading. *University of Chicago
Supplementary Educational Monographs,* 1953, *77,* 9-28.

Robinson, Helen M. Perceptual and conceptual style related to reading.

In J. A. Figurel (Ed.), Improvement of reading through classroom practice. *Proceedings of the International Reading Association,* 1964, *9,* 26-28.

Robinson, Helen M., & Smith, Helen K. Reading clinic clients—ten years after. *Elementary School Journal,* 1962, *63,* 22-27.

Robinson, Helen M., Weintraub, S., & Smith, Helen K. Summary of investigations relating to reading. July 1, 1965 to June 30, 1966. *Reading Research Quarterly,* 1966-67, *2*(2), 1-141.

Roman, M. *Reaching delinquents through reading.* Springfield, Ill.: Charles C. Thomas, 1957.

Rorschach, H. *Psychodiagnostic plates.* New York: The Psychological Corp., n. d.

Rosen, C. L. Visual deficiencies and reading disability. In A. J. Kingston (Ed.), Research for the classroom. *Journal of Reading,* 1965, *9,* 57-61.

Roswell, Florence, & Natchez, Gladys. *Reading disability: diagnosis and treatment.* New York: Basic Books, 1964.

Russell, D. H., & Fea, H. R. Research on teaching reading. In N. L. Gage (Ed.), *Handbook of research on teaching.* Chicago: Rand McNally, 1963. Pp. 865-928.

Rutherford, W. L. The effects of a perceptual-motor training program on the performance of kindergarten pupils on Metropolitan Reading Readiness Tests. Unpublished doctoral dissertation, North Texas State University, 1964.

Ryan, Elizabeth M. A comparative study of the achievement of second-grade pupils in programs characterized by a contrasting degree of parent participation. Unpublished doctoral dissertation, Indiana University, 1964.

Sawyer, Rita I. Does the Wechsler Intelligence Scale for Children discriminate between mildly disabled and severely disabled readers? *Elementary School Journal,* 1965, *66,* 97-103.

Schiffman, G. Dyslexia as an educational phenomenon: its recognition and treatment. In J. Money (Ed.), *Reading disability: progress and research needs in dyslexia.* Baltimore: Johns Hopkins Press, 1962. Pp. 45-60.

Schiffman, G. Early identification of reading disabilities: the responsibility of the public school. *Bulletin of the Orton Society,* 1964, *14,* 42-44.

Schneyer, J. W. Use of the cloze procedure for improving reading comprehension. *The Reading Teacher,* 1965, *19,* 174-79.

Schonell, F. J. *The psychology and teaching of reading.* (4th ed.) London: Oliver & Boyd, 1961.

Schwyhart, F. K. Exploration of the self-concept of retarded readers in relation to reading achievement. Unpublished doctoral dissertation, University of Arizona, 1967.

Shaw, M. C., Edson, K., & Bell, H. M. The self-concept of bright underachieving high school students as revealed by an adjective check list. *Personnel and Guidance Journal*, 1960, *39*, 193-96.

Sheldon, M. S., & Garton, Jeanette. A note on "a WISC profile for retarded readers." *Alberta Journal of Educational Research*, 1959, *5*, 264-67.

Sheldon, W. D., & Carillo, L. Relation of parents, home, and developmental characteristics to children's reading ability. *Elementary School Journal*, 1952, *52*, 262-70.

Shimota, Helen E. Reading skills in emotionally disturbed institutionalized adolescents. *Journal of Educational Research*, 1964, *58*, 106-11.

Shipp, D. E., & Loudon, Mary L. The Draw-a-Man Test and achievement in the first grade. *Journal of Educational Research*, 1964, *57*, 518-21.

Silver, A. A., & Hagin, Rosa A. Specific reading disability, delineation of the syndrome and relationship to cerebral dominance. *Comprehensive Psychiatry*, 1960, *1*, 126-34.

Silver, A. A., & Hagin, Rosa A. Specific reading disability: a twelve-year follow-up study. *American Journal of Orthopsychiatry*, 1963, *33*, 338-39.

Silver, A. A., & Hagin, Rosa A. Maturation of perceptual functions in children with specific reading disability. *The Reading Teacher*, 1966, *19*, 253-59.

Silverman, Charlotte (Chm.) Psychological development of culturally disadvantaged Negro kindergarten children: a study of the selective influences of family and school variables. *American Journal of Orthopsychiatry*, 1967, *37*, 367-68.

Silverman, J. S., Fite, Margretta W., & Mosher, Margaret M. Clinical findings in reading disability children: special cases of intellectual inhibition. *American Journal of Orthopsychiatry*, 1959, *29*, 298-314.

Smith, Carol E., & Keogh, Barbara K. The group Bender-Gestalt as a reading readiness screening instrument. *Perceptual and Motor Skills*, 1962, *15*, 639-45.

Spache, G. D. *Toward better reading*. Champaign, Ill.: Garrard, 1963.

Spache, G. D., & Tillman, C. E. A comparison of the visual profiles of retarded and non-retarded readers. *Journal of Developmental Reading*, 1962, *5*, 101-08.

Speasl, Dorothy, & Herrington, Jewell. A study of socio-economic level and reading success in a school with a changing population. *Illinois School Research*, 1965, *2*, 27-31.

Staiger, R. C. Medicine for reading improvement. *Journal of Developmental Reading,* 1961, *5,* 48-51.

Stevens, W. E., Cunningham, E. S., & Stigler, B. J. Reading readiness and eye-hand preference patterns in first-grade children. *Exceptional Children,* 1967, *33,* 481-88.

Stott, D. H. Infantile illness and subsequent mental and emotional development. *Journal of Genetic Psychology,* 1959, *94,* 233-51.

Strang, Ruth. Relationships between certain aspects of intelligence and certain aspects of reading. *Educational and Psychological Measurement,* 1943, *3,* 355-59.

Strang, Ruth. *Diagnostic teaching of reading.* New York: McGraw-Hill, 1964.

Strang, Ruth. Diagnostic teaching of reading in high school. *Journal of Reading,* 1965, *8,* 147-54. (a)

Strang, Ruth. The reading process and its ramifications. In *Tenth Annual Convention, International Reading Association Invitational Addresses 1965.* Newark, Delaware: International Reading Association, 1965. Pp. 48-73. (b)

Strang, Ruth, McCullough, Constance M., & Traxler, A. E. *The Improvement of reading.* (4th ed.) New York: McGraw-Hill, 1967.

Strickler, E. Educational group counseling within a remedial reading program. Unpublished doctoral dissertation, University of Southern California, 1964.

Stuart, I. R. Perceptual style and reading ability: implications for an instructional approach. *Perceptual and Motor Skills,* 1967, *24,* 135-38.

Sutton, M. H. Readiness for reading at the kindergarten level. *The Reading Teacher,* 1964, *17,* 234-40.

Swales, T. D. The attainments in reading and spelling of children who learned to read through the initial teaching alphabet. *British Journal of Educational Psychology,* 1967, *37,* 126-27.

Talmadge, M., Davids, A., & Laufer, M. W. A study of experimental methods for teaching emotionally disturbed, brain-damaged, retarded readers. *Journal of Educational Research,* 1963, *56,* 311-16.

Terman, L. M., & Merrill, M. A. *Stanford-Binet intelligence scale, from L-M.* Boston: Houghton Mifflin, 1960.

Thompson, Bertha B. A longitudinal study of auditory discrimination. *Journal of Educational Research,* 1963, *56,* 376-78.

Thorpe, L. P., Lefever, D. W., & Haslund, R. *SRA Achievement series: reading.* Chicago: Science Research Associates, Inc., 1954-64.

Tinker, M. A. Recent studies of eye movements in reading. *Psychological Bulletin,* 1958, *54,* 215-31.

Traxler, A. E. Problems of group remedial reading in the secondary school. *Education Digest*, 1939, *4*, 25-28.

Traxler, A. E. Problems of measurement in reading. *Proceedings of the 1941 Invitational Conference on Testing Problems*, American Council on Education, 1941, 66-73. (Mimeo.)

Valusek, J. E. The effect of drugs on retarded readers in a state mental hospital. Unpublished doctoral dissertation, University of Michigan, 1963.

Van de Rift, V., & De Rift, H. Visual motor coordination in underachieving and normal school boys. *Perceptual and Motor Skills*, 1964, *19*, 731-34.

Van Zandt, W. A study of some home-family community factors related to children's achievement in reading in an elementary school. Unpublished doctoral dissertation, Wayne State University, 1963.

Vernon, M. D. Symposium: contributions to the diagnosis and remedial treatment of reading difficulties. *British Journal of Educational Psychology*, 1960, *30*, 146-54.

Vernon, P. E. Dullness and its causes. *New York Times Educational Supplement*, October 26, 1956.

Vernon, P. E. Education and the psychology of individual differences. *Harvard Educational Review*, 1958, *28*, 91-104.

Vernon, P. E. The determinants of reading comprehension. *Educational and Psychological Measurement*, 1962, *22*, 269-86.

Vorhaus, Pauline G. Rorschach configurations associated with reading disability. *Journal of Projective Techniques*, 1952, *16*, 2-19.

Waldstreicher, J. S. Eye-movement photography, an effective diagnostic aid. *Optical Journal and Review of Optometry*, 1966, *103*, 23-27.

Walters, R. H., & Doan, Helen. Perceptual and cognitive functioning of retarded readers. *Journal of Consulting Psychology*, 1962, *26*, 355-61.

Walters, R. H., & Kosowski, Irene. Symbolic learning and reading retardation. *Journal of Consulting Psychology*, 1963, *27*, 75-82.

Walters, R. H., Van Loan, Malle, & Crofts, Irene. A study of reading disability. *Journal of Consulting Psychology*, 1961, *25*, 277-83

Watson, R. L. An analysis of nine selected factors relating to good and poor readers in the sixth grade to dropping out before the completion of high school. Unpublished doctoral dissertation, Indiana University, 1964.

Wechsler, D. *Wechsler intelligence scale for children*. New York: The Psychological Corp., 1949.

Wechsler, D. *Wechsler adult intelligence scale.* New York: The Psychological Corp., 1955.

Wechsler, D. *The Wechsler Primary and Pre-school Scale of Intelligence.* New York: The Psychological Corp., 1966.

Weeks, E. E. The effect of specific pre-reading materials on children's performances on the Murphy-Durrell Diagnostic Reading Readiness Test. Unpublished doctoral dissertation, University of Connecticut, 1964.

Western Psychological Services. *The visual Gestalt test two, copy drawing form.* Beverly Hills, Calif.: Author, 1964.

Weiner, Bluma B. Assessment: beyond psychometry. *Exceptional Children,* 1967, *33,* 367-70.

Weitzner, M., Stallone F., & Smith, G. M. Personality profiles of high, middle, and low MAS subjects. *Journal of Psychology,* 1967, *65,* 163-68.

Wepman, J. M. Auditory discrimination, speech, and reading. *Elementary School Journal,* 1960, *60,* 325-33.

Wepman, J. M. Dyslexia: its relationship to language acquisition and concept formation. In J. Money (Ed.), *Reading disability: progress and research needs in dyslexia.* Baltimore: Johns Hopkins Press, 1962. Pp. 179-86.

Wepman, J. M. *Wepman Auditory Discrimination Test.* Chicago: Language Research Associates, 1958.

Westover, F. L. A comparison of listening and reading as a means of testing. *Journal of Educational Research,* 1958, *52,* 23-26.

Whipple, G., & Black, M. H. *Reading for children without: our disadvantaged youth.* Newark, Delaware: International Reading Association, 1966.

Winkler, R. C., Teigland, J. J., Munger, P. F., & Kranzler, G. O. The effects of selected counseling and remedial techniques on underachieving elementary school students. *Journal of Consulting Psychology,* 1965, *12,* 384-87.

Winkley, Carol K. Building staff competence in identifying underachievers. In H. A. Robinson (Ed.), The underachiever in reading. *University of Chicago Supplementary Educational Monographs,* 1962, *92,* 155-62.

Winter Haven Lions Club, Publications Committee. *Perceptual forms test.* Winter Haven, Florida: Research Foundation, Inc., 1955-63.

Witty, P. A., & Sizemore, R. A. Studies in listening: I—Relative values of oral and visual presentation. *Elementary English,* 1958, *35,* 538-52.

Witty, P. A., & Sizemore, R. A. Studies in listening: II—Relative values of oral and visual presentation. *Elementary English,* 1959, *36,* 59-70.

Witty, P. A., & Sizemore, R. A. Studies in listening: III—Relative values of oral and visual presentation. *Elementary English,* 1959, *36,* 130-40.

Woodbury, C. A. The identification of underachieving readers. *The Reading Teacher,* 1963, *16,* 218-23.

Woolf, M. D. The TAT and reading disability. In E. P. Bliesmer & R. C. Staiger (Eds.), Problems, programs, and projects in college-adult reading. *Eleventh Yearbook of the National Reading Conference,* 1962, *11,* 180-88.

Young, F. A. Reading, measures of intelligence and refractive errors. *American Journal of Optometry and Archives of American Academy of Optometry,* 1963, *40,* 257-64.

ADDITIONAL SOURCES

Alexander, D., & Money, J. Reading disability and the problem of direction sense. *The Reading Teacher,* 1967, *20,* 404-09.

Ammons, R. B., & Ammons, C. H. The Quick Test (QT): provisional manual. *Psychological Report: Monograph Supplement,* 1962, *11,* 111-61.

Anderson, H. E., Jr. The prediction of reading and language from the California tests. *Educational and Psychological Measurement,* 1961, *21,* 1035-36.

Balow, I. H., & Balow, B. Lateral dominance and reading achievement in the second grade. *American Educational Research Journal,* 1964, *1,* 139-43.

Bereiter, C., & Engelmann, S. *Teaching disadvantaged children in the preschool.* Englewood Cliffs, N. J.: Prentice-Hall, 1966.

Blackman, L. S., & Holden, E. A., Jr. Support vs. non-support in an autoinstructional word program for educable retardates. *American Journal of Mental Deficiency,* 1963, *67,* 592-600.

Bliesmer, E. P. Evaluating progress in remedial reading programs. *The Reading Teacher,* 1962, *15,* 344-50.

Broom, M. E. *Effective reading instruction.* New York: McGraw-Hill, 1961.

Bryant, N. D. Some principles of remedial instruction for dyslexia. *The Reading Teacher,* 1965, *18,* 567-72.

Caffrey, J. G., & Michael, W. B. Auding. *Review of Educational Research,* 1955, *25,* 121-38.

Chansky, N. M. Threat, anxiety, and reading behavior. *Journal of Educational Research,* 1958, *51,* 333-40.

Charles, H. A selected drug as determinant in the reading process. *Journal of the Reading Specialist,* 1966, *5,* 154-55, 170.

Cleland, D. L. Clinical materials for appraising disabilities in reading. *The Reading Teacher,* 1964, *17,* 428-34.

Cleland, D. L., & Toussaint, Isabella H. The interrelationships of reading, listening, arithmetic computation, and intelligence. *The Reading Teacher,* 1962, *15,* 228-31.

Cohn, R. Delayed acquisition of reading and writing abilities in children. *Archives of Neurology,* 1961, *4,* 153-61.

Combs, A. W., & Snygg, D. *Individual behavior.* New York: Harper, 1959.

Combs, R.H., & Harper, J. L. Effects of labels on attitudes of educators toward handicapped children. *Exceptional Children, 1967, 33,* 399-403.

Critchley, M. *Developmental dyslexia.* Springfield, Ill.: Charles C. Thomas, 1964.

Daley, W. T. (Ed.) *Speech and language therapy with brain-damaged child.* Washington, D. C.: Catholic University of America Press, 1962.

Deal, Margaret. A summary of research concerning patterns of wisc sub-test scores of retarded readers. *Journal of the Reading Specialist, 1965, 4,* 101-11.

de Hirsch, Katrina, Jansky, Jeannette J., & Langford, W. S. *The prediction of reading, spelling, and writing disabilities in children: a preliminary study.* New York: Columbia University, 1965.

Delacato, Carl H. *The diagnosis and treatment of speech and reading problems.* Springfield, Ill.: Charles C. Thomas, 1963.

Dolch, E. W. How to diagnose children's reading difficulties by informal classroom techniques. *The Reading Teacher,* 1953, *6,* 10-14.

Durrell, D. D., Murphy, Helen A., & Sullivan, Helen B. *Building word power in primary reading.* Yonkers-on-Hudson, N. Y.: World Book, 1945.

Durrell, D. D., & Murphy, Helen A. *Speech-to-print phonics.* New York: Harcourt, Brace & World, 1964.

English, H. B., & English, Ava C. *A comprehensive dictionary of psychological and psychoanalytical terms.* New York: Longmans, Green & Co., 1958.

Feldmann, Shirley. Predicting early success. In J. A. Figurel (Ed.), Reading and inquiry. *International Reading Association Conference Proceedings,* 1965, *10,* 408-10.

Flescher, I. Ocular manual laterality and perceptual rotation of literal symbols. *Genetic Psychology Monographs,* 1962, *66,* 3-48.

Gardner, R. W., & Lohrenz, I. J. Attention and assimilation. *American Journal of Psychology,* 1961, *74,* 607-11.

Garlock, J., Dollarhide, R. S., & Hopkins, K. D. Comparability of scores on the Wide Range and the Gilmore Oral Reading tests. *California Journal of Educational Research,* 1965, *16,* 54-57.

Geake, R. R. Predictors of reading rate improvement. In *The interinstitutional seminar in child development, collected papers.* Dearborn, Mich.: Edison Institute, 1963.

Gellert, Elizabeth. Systematic observation: a method of child study. *Harvard Educational Review,* 1955, *25,* 179-95.

Gesell, A., Ilg, Frances L., & Bullis, Glenna E. *Vision: its development in infant and child.* New York: Harper & Row, 1950.

Gibson, Eleanor J., Gibson, J. J., Pick, Anne D., & Osser, H. A developmental study of the discrimination of letter-like forms. *Journal of Comparative and Physiological Psychology,* 1962, *55,* 897-906.

Gibson, J. J., & Gibson, Eleanor J. Perceptual learning: differentiation or enrichment? *Psychological Review,* 1955, *66,* 32-41.

Goetzinger, C. P., Dirks, D. D., & Baer, C. J. Auditory discrimination and visual perception in good and poor readers. *Annals of Otology, Rhinology, and Laryngology,* 1960, *69,* 121-36.

Gorelick, M. C. Effectiveness of visual form training in a pre-reading program. *Journal of Educational Research,* 1965, *58,* 315-18.

Gould, L. M. Visual perception training. *Elementary School Journal,* 1967, *67,* 381-89.

Hafner, L. E. Cloze procedure In A. J. Kingston (Ed.), Research for the classroom teacher. *Journal of Reading,* 1966, *9,* 415-21.

Hewett, F. M. A hierarchy of educational tasks for children with learning disorders. *Exceptional Children,* 1964, *31,* 207-14.

Hitchcock, A. A., & Alfred, Cleo. Can teacher make accurate estimates of reading ability? *Clearing House,* 1955, *29,* 422-23.

Jampolsky, G. G. Psychiatric considerations in reading disorders. In R. M. Fowler, Helen F. Golman, & Lucie L. Lawson (Eds.), *Reading disorders.* Philadelphia: F. A. Davis, 1965. Pp. 61-72.

King, Ethel M. Effects of different kinds of visual discrimination training on learning to read words. *Journal of Educational Psychology,* 1964, *55,* 325-33.

Koppitz Elizabeth M. The Bender Gestalt test and learning disturbances in young children. *Journal of Clinical Psychology,* 1958, *14,* 292-95.

Lachmann, F. M. Perceptual motor development in children retarded in reading ability. *Journal of Consulting Psychology,* 1960, *24,* 427-31.

Lanning, F. W., & Many, W. A. (Eds.) *Basic education for the disadvantaged adult.* Boston: Houghton Mifflin, 1966.

Lansky, L. M. Pattern of defense against conflict. Unpublished doctoral dissertation, University of Michigan, 1956.

Libaw, Frieda, Berres, Frances, & Coleman, J. C. A new method for evaluating the effectiveness of treatment of learning difficulties. *Journal of Educational Research,* 1962, *55,* 582-84.

Llorens, Lela A., Rubin, E. Z., Braun, Jean, Beck, Gayle, Mottley, N., & Beall, D. Cognitive-perceptual-motor functions. *American Journal of Occupational Therapy,* 1964, *18,* 202-08.

Lockhard, Joan, & Sidowski, J. B. Learning in fourth and sixth graders as a function of sensory mode of stimulus presentation and overt or covert practice. *Journal of Educational Psychology,* 1961, *52,* 262-65.

Loughlin, L. J., O'Connor, H. A., Powell, M., & Parsley, K. M., Jr. An investigation of sex differences by intelligence, subject-matter area, grade and achievement level of three anxiety scales. *Journal of Genetic Psychology,* 1965, *106,* 207-15.

Malpass, L. F., Hardy, M. W., Gilmore, M. A., & Williams, C. F. Automated instruction for retarded children. *American Journal of Mental Deficiency,* 1964, *69,* 405-12.

McCarthy, J. J., & Olson, J. L. *Validity studies on the Illinois Test of Psycholinguistic Abilities.* Urbana, Ill.: University of Illinois Press, 1964.

McDonald, A. S. (Ed.) Research for the classroom: reading potential: appraisal or prediction? *Journal of Reading,* 1964, *8,* 115-19.

McDonald, A. S. (Ed.) Research for the classroom: using standardized tests to determine reading proficiency. *Journal of Reading,* 1964, *8,* 58-61.

Menninger, K. Psychiatrists use dangerous words. *The Saturday Evening Post,* 1964, *237* (16), 12-14.

Money, J., Walker, H. T., Jr., & Alexander, D. Development of direction sense and three syndromes of impairment. *The Slow-learning Child,* 1965, *11,* 145-55.

Morrison, H. E., & Collister, E. G. The use of difference scores in the interpretation of test results in elementary schools. *Kansas University Bulletin of Education,* 1961, *16,* 19-25.

Moustakas, C. E. *The authentic teacher.* Cambridge, Mass.: Howard A. Doyle, 1966

Orton, S. T. *Reading, writing, and speech disorders in children: a presentation of certain types of disorders in the development of the language faculty.* New York: W. W. Norton, 1937.

Orton Society. Papers presented in the section on special language disability at the *Forty-second Annual Convention of the Council for Exceptional Children—Monograph,* 1964, *1,* 1-95.

Radlow, R. Patterning of reinforcement in aversive training. Unpublished doctoral dissertation, Pennsylvania State Universtiy, 1955.

Radner, S. Combining group guidance and the language arts. *High Points,* 1956, *38,* 64-67.

Reger, R. *School psychology.* Springfield, Ill.: Charles C. Thomas, 1965

Robbins, M. P. The Delacato interpretation of neurological organization: an empirical study. Unpublished doctoral dissertation. University of Chicago, 1965.

Robbins, M. P. The Delacato interpretation of neurological organization. *Reading Research Quarterly,* 1966, *1* (3), 57-78.

Robbins, M. P. Study of the validity of Delacato's theory of neurological organization. *Exceptional Child,* 1966, *33,* 199-202; 1966, *32,* 517-23.

Robeck, Mildred C. Effect of laboratory experience on course work in the teaching of remedial reading. *California Journal of Educational Research,* 1962, *13,* 154-59.

Robeck, Mildred C. Readers who lacked word analysis skills: a group diagnosis. *Journal of Educational Research,* 1963, *56,* 432-34.

Roberts, R. W., & Coleman, J. C. An investigation of the role of visual and kinesthetic factors in reading failure. *Journal of Educational Research,* 1958, *51,* 445-51.

Roughton, E. L. Creativity as a factor in reading achievement. Unpublished doctoral dissertation, University of South Carolina, 1963.

Sarason, S., Davidson, K. S., Lighthall, F. F., Waite, R. R., & Ruebush, B. K. *Anxiety in elementary school children.* New York: John Wiley, 1960.

Sheldon, W. D. Specific principles essential to classroom diagnosis. *The Reading Teacher,* 1960, *14,* 2-8.

Sheppard, C., & Campbell, W. J. An evaluation of the California Achievement Test, Elementary, Form W, Reading Vocabulary. *Journal of Educational Research,* 1963, *56,* 481-82.

Singer, H., & Clymer, T. Substrata-factor evaluation of a precocious reader. *The Reading Teacher,* 1965, *18,* 288.

Smith, D. E. P., & Carrigan, Patricia M. *The nature of reading disability.* New York: Harcourt Brace, 1959.

Smith, Helen K. *Instruction of high school students in reading for different purposes.* (Cooperative Research Project No. 1714, Office of Education, United States Department of Health, Education, and Welfare.) Chicago: University of Chicago Press, 1966.

Solan, H. A. Some physiological correlates of dyslexia. *American Journal of Optometry and Archives of American Academy of Optometry,* 1966, *43* (1), 3-9.

Spache, G. D. What teachers should know about vision and reading. *Optometric Weekly,* 1966, *57,* 27-31.

Spradlin, J. E. Assessment of speech and language of retarded children: the Parsons Language Sample. *Journal of Speech and Hearing Disorders Monograph Supplement,* 1963, No. 10, 8-31, 81-91.

Stemmler, Ann. Reading of highly creative versus highly intelligent secondary students. Unpublished doctoral dissertation, University of Chicago, 1966.

Stephens, W. E., Cunningham, E. S., & Stigler, B. J. Reading readiness and eye-hand preference patterns in first-grade children. *Exceptional Children,* 1967, *33,* 481-88.

Strauss, A. A., & Lehtinen, Laura E. *Psychopathology and education of the brain-injured child.* Vol. 1. New York: Grune and Stratton, 1947.

Symons, W. J. The relationships of instruction in initial phonetic elements to the reading achievement of remedial reading pupils. Unpublished doctoral dissertation, University of California at Berkeley, 1964.

Townsend, Agatha. What research says to the reading teacher: applied reading—a bibliography. *The Reading Teacher,* 1962, *16,* 189-91, 193-94, 201.

Tracy, R. J., & Rankin, E. E. Methods of computing and evaluating residual gain scores in the reading program. *Journal of Reading,* 1967, *10,* 363-71.

Traxler, A. E. Correlation between achievement scores and school marks in an independent school for boys. *Journal of Applied Psychology,* 1940, *24,* 58-63.

Usdan, M. D., & Bertolaet, F. (Eds.). *Teachers for the disadvantaged.* Chicago: Follett, 1966.

Vernon, M. D. *Backwardness in reading. A study of its nature and origin.* London: Cambridge University Press, 1960.

Vernon, P. E. The relation of intelligence to educational backwardness. *Educational Review,* 1958, *11,* 7-15.

Vorhaus, Pauline G. Personality seen in children with reading problems and in adults with corresponding problems. *National Association of Women Deans and Counselors Journal,* 1961, *24,* 104-05.

Webster, S. W. (Ed.) *The disadvantaged learner: knowing, understanding, educating.* San Francisco: Chandler, 1966.

Weener, P., Barrett, L. S., & Semmel, M. I. A response: J. J. McCarthy—A critical evaluation of the Illinois Test of Psycholinguistic Abilities. *Exceptional Children,* 1967, *33,* 373-82.

Wepman, J. M. *A selected bibliography on brain impairment, aphasia, and organic psychodiagnosis.* Chicago: Language Research Associates, 1961.

Whitsell, L. J. Neurological aspects of reading disorders. In R. M. Flower, Helen Grofman, & Lucie L. Lawson (Eds.), *Reading disorders.* Philadelphia: F. A. Davis, 1965. Pp. 45-60.

Williams, Joanna P., & Levin, H. Word perception: psychological bases. *Education,* 1967, *87,* 515-18.

Worley, S. E., & Story, W. E. Socio-economic status and language facility of beginning first graders. *The Reading Teacher,* 1967, *20,* 400-03.

Zangwill, O. L. Dyslexia in relation to cerebral dominance. In J. Money (Ed.), *Reading disability: progress and research needs in dyslexia.* Baltimore: Johns Hopkins Press, 1962. Pp. 103-13.

Zintz, Miles V. *Corrective reading.* Dubuque, Iowa: Wm. C. Brown Co., 1966.

TEST APPENDIX

Basic sight word test. W. E. DOLCH. Champaign, Ill.: Garrard Press, 1942. (Grades 1-2)

Bender Gestalt test. G. R. PASCAL & BARBARA J. SUTTELL. New York: Grune & Stratton, Inc., 1951. (Ages 4 and over)

Bender revised Gestalt test. M. L. HUTT & G. J. BRISKIN. New York: Grune & Stratton, Inc., 1960. (Ages 7 and over)

Bender visual motor Gestalt test. LAURETTA BENDER. New York: American Orthopsychiatric Assn., Inc., 1938-46. (Ages 4 and over)

Bender visual motor Gestalt test for children. AILEEN CLAWSON. Beverly Hills, Calif.: Western Psychological Services, 1962. (Ages 7-11)

Bender Gestalt test for young children. ELIZABETH M. KOPPITZ. New York: Grune & Stratton, Inc., 1964. (Ages 5-10)

Brown-Carlsen listening comprehension test: evaluation and adjustment series. J. I. BROWN & G. R. CARLSEN, New York: Harcourt, Brace & World, Inc., 1953-55. (Grades 9-13)

Chicago visual discrimination test. J. M. WEPMAN, *et al.* Chicago: University of Chicago Press, 1967.

Children's drawings as measures of intellectual maturity: a revision and extention of the Goodenough draw-a-man test. FLORENCE L. GOODENOUGH & D. B. HARRIS. New York: Harcourt, Brace and World, 1963.

Closure flexibility (concealed figures). L. L. THURSTONE & T. E. JEFFREY. Chicago: University of Chicago, Education-Industry Service, 1956-63. (For industrial employees)

Cooperative English tests: reading comprehension. C. DERRICK, D. P. HARRIS, & B. WALKER. Princeton, N. J.: Cooperative Test Division, Educational Testing Service, 1960.

Cooperative vocabulary test. F. B. DAVIS, *et al.* Princeton, N. J.: Cooperative Test Division, Educational Testing Service, 1940-53. (Grades 7-16)

Crichton vocabulary scale. J. C. RAVEN. London: H. K. Lewis & Co., Ltd., 1950. (Ages 4-11)

Davis reading test. F. B. DAVIS & CHARLOTTE C. DAVIS. New York: Psychological Corp., 1956-62. (Grades 8-11, 11-13)

Detroit tests of learning aptitude. H. J. BAKER & BERNICE LE-LAND. Indianapolis: Bobbs Merrill Co., 1935-55. (Ages 3 and over)

Diagnostic reading tests, survey section, auditory comprehension. COMMITTEE ON DIAGNOSTIC READING TESTS. Mountain Home, N. C.: Author, 1957-63. (Grades K-4)

Differential aptitude tests. G. K. BENNETT, H. G. SEASHORE, & A. G. WESMAN. New York: Psychological Corp., 1947-63. (Grades 8-13 and adults)

Durrell analysis of reading difficulty. D. D. DURRELL. New York: Harcourt, Brace & World, 1937-55. Grades 1-6)

Embedded figures test. H. A. WITKIN. Brooklyn, N. Y.: Witkin State University College of Medicine, 1950-62. (Ages 10 and over)

Examining for aphasia: a manual for the examination of aphasia and related disturbances. J. EISENSON. New York: Psychological Corp., 1946-54.

Frostig developmental test of visual perception. MARIANNE FROSTIG, D. W. LEFEVER, J. WHITTLESEY, & PHYLLIS MASLOW. Palo Alto, Calif.: Consulting Psychologist Press, 1961-64. (Ages 3-8)

Gates reading readiness tests. A. I. GATES. New York: Bureau of Publications, Teachers College, Columbia University, 1939-42. (Grade 1)

Gilmore oral reading test. J. V. GILMORE. New York: Harcourt, Brace & World, 1951-52. (Grades 1-8)

Graded word reading test, test RI. F. J. SCHONELL. Edinburgh, Scotland: Oliver Boyd, Ltd., 1942. (Ages 5-15)

Gray oral reading test. HELEN M. ROBINSON & W. S. GRAY. Indianapolis: Bobbs Merrill Co., 1963. (Grades 1-16 and adults)

Harris test of lateral dominance. A. J. HARRIS. New York: Psychological Corp., 1947-58.

Harrison-Stroud reading readiness profiles. M. LUCILLE HARRISON & J. B. STROUD. Boston: Houghton Mifflin Company, 1949-56. (Grades K-1)

Illinois test of psycholinguistic abilities (experimental edition). J. J.

McCARTHY & S. A. KIRK. Urbana, Ill.: University of Illinois Press, 1961-63.

Leavell hand-eye coordinator tests. U. W. LEAVELL. Meadville, Pa.: Keystone View Company, 1958. (Ages 8-14)

Lee-Clark reading readiness test (revised). J. M. LEE & W. W. CLARK. Monterey, Calif.: California Test Bureau, 1962. (Grades K-1)

Listening. MARGARET J. EARLY, *et al.* Princeton, N. J.: Cooperative Test Division, Educational Testing Service, 1956-57.

Lorge-Thorndike intelligence tests. I. LORGE & R. L. THORNDIKE. Boston: Houghton Mifflin, 1954-62. (Grades K-1, 2-3, 4-6, 7-9, 10-12)

McCullough word analysis tests. CONSTANCE M. McCULLOUGH. Boston: Ginn, 1962-63. (Grades 4-6)

Memory-for-designs test. F. K. GRAHAM & BARBARA S. KENDALL. Missoula, Mont.: Psychological Test Specialists, 1946-60. (Ages 8.5 and over)

Mental health analysis. L. P. THORPE & W. W. CLARK. Monterey, Calif.: California Test Bureau, 1946-59.

Metropolitan readiness tests. GERTRUDE H. HILDRETH & NELLIE GRIFFITHS. New York: Harcourt, Brace & World, 1933-50. (Grades K-1)

Metropolitan reading achievement tests. W. DUROST, H. BIXLER, GERTRUDE HILDRETH, K. LUND, & J. W. WRIGHTSTONE. New York: Harcourt, Brace & World, 1932-62. (Four levels)

Minnesota percepto-diagnostic test. G. B. FULLER & J. T. LAIRD. Brandon, Vt.: Journal of Clinical Psychology, 1962-63. (Ages 8-15, 18-65)

Monroe reading aptitude test. MARIAN MONROE. Boston: Houghton Mifflin, 1935. (Grades K-1)

Murphy-Durrell diagnostic reading readiness test. HELEN A. MURPHY & D. D. DURRELL. New York: Harcourt, Brace & World, 1947-49.

Non-language multi-mental test. E. L. TERMAN, W. McCALL, & I. LORGE. New York: Bureau of Publications, Teachers College, Columbia University, 1942. (Grades 2 and over)

Peabody picture vocabulary test. L. M. DUNN. Minneapolis: American Guidance Service, 1959. (Ages 2.5-18)

Perceptual forms test. WINTER HAVEN LIONS CLUB. Winter Haven, Fla.: Winter Haven Lions Research Foundation, Inc., 1955-63. (Ages 6-8.5)

Pictorial test of intelligence. J. L. FRENCH. Boston: Houghton Mifflin, 1964. (Ages 3-8)

The quick test. R. B. AMMONS & C. H. AMMONS. Missoula, Mont.: Psychological Test Specialists, 1958-62. (Ages 2 and over)

Robbins speech-sound discrimination and verbal imagery type tests. S. D. ROBBINS & ROSA S. ROBBINS. Magnolia, Mass.; Expression Company, 1948-58. (Ages 4-8, 8 and over)

Sequential tests of educational progress: listening. COOPERATIVE TEST DIVISION, EDUCATIONAL TESTING SERVICE. Princeton, N. J.: Author, 1956-63.

Sequential tests of educational progress: reading. H. ALPERT, *et al.* Princeton, N. J.: Cooperative Test Division, Educational Testing Service, 1956-63.

SRA achievement series: reading. L. P. THORPE, D. W. LEFEVER, & R. HASLUND, Chicago: Science Research Associates, Inc., 1954-64. (Grades 1-9)

Stanford-Binet intelligence scale. L. M. TERMAN & MAUD A. MERRILL. Boston: Houghton Mifflin, 1916-60. (Ages 2 and over)

Thurstone's test of mental alertness. THELMA THURSTONE & L. L. THURSTONE. Chicago: Science Research Associates, Inc., 1943-53. (Grades 9-12 and adults)

The visual motor Gestalt test two, copy drawing form. WESTERN PSYCHOLOGICAL SERVICES. Beverly Hills, Calif.: Author, 1964

Wechsler adult intelligence scale. D. WECHSLER. New York: The Psychological Corp., 1955.

Wechsler intelligence scale for children. D. WECHSLER. New York: The Psychological Corp., 1949.

Wechsler pre-school and primary scale of intelligence. D. WECHSLER.
    New York: The Psychological Corp., 1966.
Wepman auditory discrimination test. J. M. WEPMAN. Chicago: Lan-
    guage Research Associates, 1958.
*Wide range achievement test: reading, spelling, arithmetic from kinder-
    garten to college.* J. JASTAK & S. BIJOU. New York: The Psy-
    chological Corp., 1940-46.

0359

Produced for the International Reading Association, Inc.
by Ray Freiman & Company
and printed by The McQuiddy Printing Co.